THE YORKSHIRE
OUSE NAVIGATION

The oil-fired steam tug OCO heading upriver through Selby Toll Bridge near the time of high water on a day in the 1950s, towing loaded barges to its owners' mills above the town. Cargoes of linseed, cottonseed, palm kernels, soya beans, copra and ground nuts were delivered to these mills, which were situated half a mile ahead, around an acute bend in the river. The mills had been built before the First World War by Joseph Watson, who had soap works in Leeds and wished to become independent of seed crushers at Hull for his supplies of oils and fats. The residues left after crushing were turned into animal feed. The factory was capable of handling over 3,000 tons of imported material per week and the company assembled a fleet of dumb barges, each with a capacity of over 200 tons, to be loaded from ships, usually in Hull docks, and towed to Selby by its own coal-fired steam tugs.

OCO (an abbreviation of Olympia Oil & Cake Mills) was one of many 65ft x 17ft TID (Tugs In Defence?) tugs speedily built during the Second World War from plates often fabricated miles away from the boatyard where they were welded together. The tugs were designed to participate in the D-day landings and to work within the Mulberry harbours. OCO was one of two of these vessels purchased after the war by Unilever, then owners of the mills, to replace their older tugs.

In 1952 British Oil & Cake Mills (BOCM) took over the plant and decided to replace the dumb craft and tugs with eighteen diesel-engined, self-propelled barges. These were built over the next eleven years by Dunstons of Thorne – the yard that built some of the company's original dumb barges as well as TID 118 which had become OCO.

In 1961, during the changeover period, OCO collided with and was sunk by the coaster MV Henfield at Swinefleet, below Goole, and after raising was rebuilt and renamed Selby Olympia for the short period of its usefulness to the company that remained.

The oil and cake mills were the largest users of the Ouse for most of the twentieth century with both ships and inland waterway craft coming to their wharves. In 1982 however, they ceased bringing cargoes upriver by barge. (Fred Harland)

2

THE YORKSHIRE OUSE NAVIGATION

Mike Taylor

TEMPUS

Tempus Publishing Limited
The Mill, Brimscombe Port,
Stroud, Gloucestershire, GL5 2QG
www.tempus-publishing.com

ISBN 0 7524 2369 X

Typesetting and origination by
Tempus Publishing Limited
Printed in Great Britain by
Midway Colour Print, Wiltshire

A postcard from the 1900s showing sailing craft moored at Queen's Staithe below Ouse Bridge in York. The very first bridge on this site was built of timber by the Romans and was replaced by a stone structure in 1275. The present crossing dates from 1860.

Contents

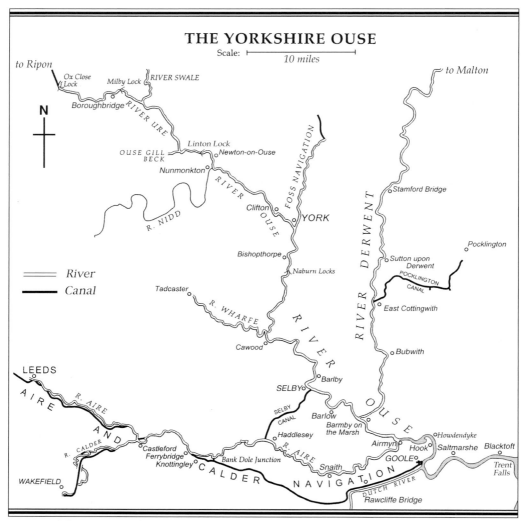

THE YORKSHIRE OUSE

Scale: |————————| 10 miles

A map of the Ouse. Hull lies on the north bank of the Humber approximately seventeen miles east of Trent Falls.

Introduction

The Yorkshire Ouse and its tributaries drain almost the whole of the county, and the river has been navigable up to York from time immemorial; indeed the Trojans are reputed to have travelled up this water highway to found the city in 980BC. Roman York was established by Agricola in 79AD and became the most important city in Britain for the next 400 years whilst Saxons, Vikings and Normans followed in their turn to capture it and all came by the same water route used by the Trojans.

The river is fifty-seven miles long and stretches from about twelve miles above York, along a twisting course, to a confluence with the River Trent at Trent Falls to form the Humber.

Edward IV appointed the Lord Mayor and Aldermen of York as Conservators of the Ouse in 1462. The ten miles below Hook, near Goole, to the start of the Humber, passed to the Aire & Calder Navigation Co. (A&CNC) in 1884 and was nationalised in 1948 along with most of the rest of Yorkshire's commercial waterways. Apart from this section, however, York City Council were responsible for almost all the river for nearly 500 years from the fifteenth century until British Waterways (BW), the nationalised authority, took it over in 1989. The short and relatively unimportant Linton Lock Navigation, above York, passed to BW in 1999, leaving them then responsible for the entire length of waterway down from Ripon.

Before these events, navigation of the Ouse had been heavily influenced by the A&CNC who opened their Selby Canal in 1778 and thus initiated a boom in the fortunes of its terminal river port, with transhipment of cargoes between 60-ton capacity canal craft and 200-ton capacity river vessels. However, within fifty years, the A&CNC had built the port of Goole and the Knottingley-Goole Canal, changing the situation again to leave Goole as the navigation's premier port.

Dates in the history of commercial navigation of the Ouse are given in the following chronology with the more important events in bold print:

1757 **A weir and lock built at Naburn, leaving the Ouse through York now non-tidal**
1769   Linton Lock (above York) completed
1772   Ripon Canal and Ure Navigation opened allowing access to Ripon via Boroughbridge
1778 **Selby Canal opened, (previously West Riding of Yorkshire linked to River Ouse and the sea only by the River Aire)**
1792   Selby Toll Bridge opened (only bridge between York and the sea)
1793   Castle Mills Lock on River Foss opened
1816   Steam packet service between Selby and Hull began (lasted until 1876)

1826 Knottingley-Goole Canal and Port of Goole opened. Most traffic to/from West Riding attracted to this route leaving only vessels trading between West Riding and York or Selby to use Selby Canal

1840 Bascule railway bridge across Ouse opened at Selby

1869 Hook Railway Swing Bridge, near Goole, opened

1870 Naburn Railway Swing Bridge opened

1872 Cawood Swing Bridge opened to replace ferry

1874 Blacktort Jetty (wood) opened to provide a mooring for craft unable to make passage between Goole and the sea on one tide

1884 A&CNC assumed responsibility for the Ouse below Goole and began improving navigation channel by construction of training walls

1885 Railway swing bridge opened at Long Drax

1888 Victoria Lock, Goole, opened improving river/docks access. Larger second lock opened at Naburn to make York accessible to deeper-draughted sea-going vessels

1889 Castle Mills Lock on River Foss rebuilt

1891 New railway swing bridge opened at Selby to replace bascule bridge of 1840

1912 West Dock, last of Goole's docks to be built, opened

1929 Boothferry Swing Bridge opened to replace last river ferry.

1938 Goole's Ocean Lock opened giving wider river/docks link

1948 Many of Britain's docks and inland waterways nationalised (not the Ouse Navigation above Hook Swing Bridge)

1956 Blacktort Jetty rebuilt in concrete

1970 Selby Toll Bridge rebuilt

1975 M62 motorway bridge, near Goole, completed

1989 Control of Ouse Navigation above Hook Swing Bridge passed to BW

1999 BW took over Linton Lock Navigation

The Ouse was tidal through York until 1757 when the first lock at Naburn was opened, making the weir there the tidal limit on most tides. Navigation on the river has always been heavily dependent on tides, with craft using the four hours before high water to have assistance from the flow when coming upriver. On neap tides, the river between Selby and York has often been short of water, especially in dry summer months and this was one of the factors in the decline of traffic to York by water, as well as the increasing popularity of cargo-carrying by road and rail during the twentieth century.

This book concentrates on the carriage of cargoes on the Ouse by both ships and inland waterway craft with an emphasis on vessels owned or built by companies based on the river. Activity at the Ouse ports of Goole, Howdendyke, Selby and York is well featured and Hull, the source and destination of much river traffic, also belongs in any book featuring a Yorkshire waterway.

Illustrations are arranged in a sequence moving upstream from Hull, with occasional diversions, in no chronological order. My own photographs and those from my collection are uncredited whilst all others are acknowledged individually. Aerial views and various types of map have been included and it is hoped that a balance has been struck between normal activity on the river during the twentieth century and examples from photographers attracted to the abundance of accidents which have occurred on the Goole-Trent Falls section and the swing bridges at Hook and Selby.

Mike Taylor.

One
Hull to Goole

Many cargoes bound for Ouse ports were loaded from ships in Alexandra or King George Dock, Hull. Here, in 1980, the motor barges *Valiant H* and *Radius* are each being loaded in King George Dock by means of grabs with a bulk cargo of over 200 tons of shea nuts for Selby out of the MV *Partnership*.

Discharge of a ship's bagged cargo by the 'rip and tip' method was an extremely labour-intensive process. Five sacks at a time were lifted out of the ship's hold using its derrick, they were then placed on deck, weighed, transferred to temporary staging fitted to the ship's side, ripped open and their contents tipped down wooden chutes into a barge's hold. Here, SS *Temple*, moored stern to the wall at the eastern end of King George Dock, is seen discharging ground nuts and palm kernels from Lagos by this means in August 1948. *(ABP)*

Floating elevators for discharge of bulk cargoes were introduced at Hull in 1955 and ships, including MV *Oriental Envoy*, are shown discharging seeds to barges in King George Dock by this method in December 1965. The view is taken looking east from atop the dock's grain silo. *(ABP)*

A large assembly of motor barges loaded with a total of over 2,500 tons of imported shea nuts for BOCM at Selby lie moored in King George Dock, Hull, prior to leaving about four hours before high water, on the 'first of flood', to deliver their cargoes to the mill or to storage sites close to the Ouse. Depending on conditions, the usual time for their Hull-Selby voyage was six hours.

Whitakers were Hull agents for Selby oil mills at one time. They also owned and operated fleets of dry cargo and tanker barges as well as tugs. Their 58ft x 14ft coal-fired steam tug *Cawood*, seen moored on the lower reaches of the River Hull (the Harbour) at Hull in 1912, shortly after the 1885-built vessel had been purchased from the Humber Pilotage Service, made many voyages up the Ouse to Selby with barges for the oil mills. (*John H. Whitaker Ltd*)

Whitakers' tug *Cawood* on trials in 1953 after conversion to diesel power by installation of a 200hp Gardner engine. The vessel was sold in 1979. (*John H. Whitaker Ltd*)

Another of Whitakers' steam tugs which worked regularly up to Selby was *Wilberforce*, built by the Yorkshire Dry Dock Co. at Hull in 1920 after that company had been taken over by Whitakers in 1918. The 62ft x 15ft vessel had the misfortune to turn onto its side twice after fouling sandbanks, once off Hull's Fish Docks in 1948 and again at Keadby on the River Trent in 1956. The vessel is shown in one of the company's River Hull dry docks after the latter incident. (*John H. Whitaker Ltd*)

In 1974, an innovative method of moving cargoes between England and mainland Europe came to the Humber as the mother ship MV *BACAT 1* began voyaging across the North Sea between Hull and Rotterdam, transporting LASH (Lighter Aboard SHip) and BACAT (Barge Aboard CATamaran) craft. Both the LASH (61½ft x 31ft x 12ft) and BACAT (55ft x 15ft x 11ft) were push-towed to Selby, Goole, and other inland ports on the Humber waterways and loaded for return to the mother ship after their cargoes had been discharged. Sadly the venture lasted only eighteen months, after industrial action was taken by Hull's dockers. Here, BW's tug *Dunheron* is shown easing two BACAT barges, one LASH barge, and the ship's stern-flow unit into *BACAT 1* at Riverside Quay, Hull, on the inaugural run of the service in March 1974. Soya beans comprised the major LASH cargo inward to Selby with scrap iron loaded for export.

The steam-powered towing barge *John M. Rishworth* on the stocks and almost complete at Henry Scarr's Hessle yard in 1915. The vessel was built for Spillers the millers and traded regularly to their mill at Selby. The vessel was converted to diesel power during its lifetime and recently became a houseboat.

The Humber Bridge, near Hessle, provided the vantage point for this photograph of Branford Barge Services' *Baysdale* heading for Hull in 1989, with a cargo of limestone loaded on the Sheffield & South Yorkshire Navigation (S&SYN) at Cadeby, near Doncaster. The barge had used the Goole-Trent Falls stretch of the Ouse to reach the Humber.

The Market Weighton Canal joined the Humber via an entrance lock two miles below Trent Falls. The waterway's major cargo comprised the export of bricks from Henry Williamson & Co.'s premises situated alongside the canal's lower reaches near Broomfleet – craft owned by them are shown waiting to load at the brickyard in the 1920s. Many cargoes were delivered to York by these craft before the 1940s, especially as the city's Tang Hall housing estate was being built in the 1920s.

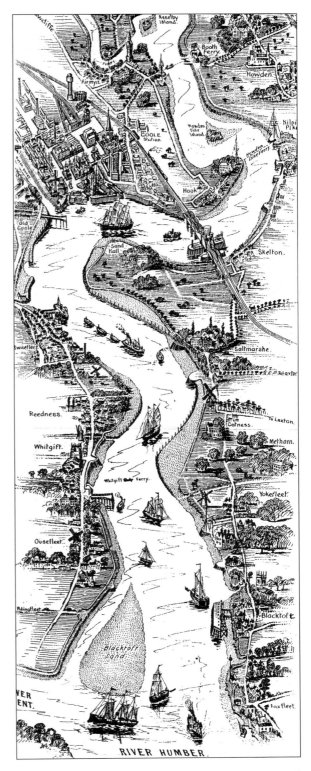

A bird's eye view of the Ouse's lower reaches drawn in 1891 showing the bank stoning then completed, three contemporary ferry crossings of the river and the layout of Goole Docks at that time. (*Courtesy of the* Yorkshire Post)

Apex Light marked the Ouse-Trent confluence after stoning of the banks of both rivers, to increase the depth of the channels, had been completed in the 1930s. Work on the Ouse had started in the mid-1890s, and by the late 1890s 2,000-ton capacity ships were reaching Goole (whereas 700-ton craft had been the maximum before). The work done was especially beneficial to the port's shipowners, permitting their vessels to operate even on neap tides. Here, in January 1976, Lincoln & Hull Marine Contractors are using their crane-barge *Linklight* to replace rotten timbers beneath the light whilst supporting it on either side with steel frames. (*Lincoln & Hull*)

Part of the Ouse training walls may be seen on the previous illustration and also on this January 1949 aerial view of the SS *Irwell*, owned at the time by British Railways and managed by Associated Humber Lines. The vessel, inward bound from Amsterdam for its home port of Goole, had discharged 700 tons of a 1,000-ton cargo at Hull and was on the last stage of its voyage when it ran aground on the Trent side of the training wall. Attempts to pull the vessel off using tugs on the next two high tides were unsuccessful, but after being stuck for thirty-six hours in the 'cradle' that it had made for itself, the ship was refloated and, leaking for'ard, completed its voyage. (*Masterman Collection*)

Blacktoft Jetty was built by the A&CNC in 1874, ten years before they took over responsibility for this section of the Ouse. Its purpose was to provide a safe mooring for vessels unable to complete their voyages to/from Goole on one tide due to fog or shortage of water in the river. For example, it was often high water over the Humber's Whitton Sands, where many craft have grounded and a few sunk as the next tide came, before a ship was able to leave Goole. Unless a fast passage could be effected, it was much safer to break the ship's voyage to the sea at Blacktoft. A crowded Blacktoft Jetty is shown on this postcard taken in the 1900s.

A clearer view of the wooden jetty at Blacktoft with the Goole & Hull Steam Packet Co.'s *Empress* or *Her Majesty* passing in the 1900s. These vessels operated a Goole-Hull passenger/small cargo service, starting in the late nineteenth century, until the First World War. With the replacement of sail by increasingly more powerful diesel engines, the locking out into the river of ships at Goole was speeded up and usage of the jetty declined. (*Masterman Collection*)

Blacktoft Jetty was rebuilt in concrete during 1956 and here, Everards' Selby-built MV *Selectivity* is lying windbound in 1992 whilst carrying part of a desulphurisation plant from Glasgow up to the power station at Drax, near Selby.

This page from the John Harker Co. Scrapbook commemorates the early 1947 Ouse freeze-up with two 100-ton capacity dumb Leeds-bound tankers, *Marjory H* and *Dorothy H*, stopped on the river above Blacktoft whilst ice was being cleared from the tug's cooling system. It was then found that the craft moved upriver with the incoming tide as fast as they had been moving when under tow. *Marjory* had recently been returned to the Humber after spending most of the Second World War in Belgium.

The City of York began to offer a towing service to and from the city in 1879 when they purchased the steam tug *Ebor Express*. This was followed by *City of York, Enterprise, Robie, Sir Joseph Rymer* and finally, in 1905, by *Lancelot*. By 1935, when this picture was taken, only the latter two remained and *Lancelot* is seen towing four barges upriver above Blacktoft in V-formation as ships head downriver. *Lancelot* worked mainly between Hull and Selby at this time, but when *Sir Joseph Rymer* was sold in 1937, it handled the remaining dumb craft bound to/from York until the service ceased in 1947.

Another incident featuring a British Railways/Associated Humber Lines ship here shows their 1,100-ton capacity SS *Aire*, built in 1930, grounded on the Ouse's north bank training wall near Saltmarshe with the launch *Pendonna* alongside, after colliding with a German freighter whilst bound for Goole from Antwerp in October 1958. A gash 60ft long was torn in its side and responsibility for the accident was subsequently apportioned 25% to *Aire* and 75% to the other vessel. *Aire* was broken up on the spot. Accidents often happened on this stretch of river when a coaster, aiming to be first in the queue to load, chose to come upriver on the 'first of flood' when there was hardly sufficient water beneath its keel to ensure proper control of the vessel. (*Norman Burnitt*)

In 1864, the Goole Steam Shipping Co. was formed. Its fleet was sold to the Lancashire & Yorkshire Railway Co. in 1905 and subsequently passed to the London & North Western Railway in 1922 and London Midland & Scottish Railway in 1924. Associated Humber Lines took over management of these 'Railway Boats' in 1935 and continued after nationalisation of the railways in 1948, until 1971. These craft easily outnumbered the other Goole-based ships. Two such vessels (*Irwell* and *Aire*) have been pictured earlier and this publicity postcard shows another; the first SS *Dearne*, built in 1909 for the L&YR and lost in the North Sea in 1915, during the First World War. A replacement 1,000-ton capacity SS *Dearne* was built for the LMS in 1924.

Associated Humber Lines' SS *Hodder*, another Railway Boat, was built in 1910 for the L&YR and had much better luck than its sister ship, the SS *Dearne*, by coming through both world wars unscathed. It is shown here heading up the Ouse to Goole in 1947 and remained in the fleet after nationalisation until 1956.

James Hargreaves & Sons (Leeds) had an extensive coal-carrying operation on the A&CN for most of the twentieth century. They also ventured into shipowning in the 1920s, with two 1,100-ton capacity vessels having low wheelhouses and hinged funnels for working under Thames bridges. One of these, the SS *Harfry*, built at Goole in 1924, is shown at anchor in the Ouse. The ship was based at Goole until it was lost following a collision off Dunkirk in December 1939.

Opening of the Goole Canal.

Notice is hereby given,

THAT THE

New Canal

FROM GOOLE TO FERRYBRIDGE,

Will be OPENED to the PUBLIC,

FOR THE

Passage of Vessels,

On Thursday next, the 20th Instant.

N. B. All Vessels which enter the Lock at Goole *upwards*, or at Ferrybridge *downwards*, on Thursday the 20th, Friday the 21st, and Saturday the 22nd Instant, will be allowed to pass, upon payment of the same Tolls as by way of Selby:—afterwards, they will be charged agreeably to the Rates under the Act of 1st. Geo. IV. for making the Goole Canal.

NAVIGATION OFFICE, WAKEFIELD, July 13th, 1826.

Providing deeper water than Selby and realising that sailing ships using that port were often delayed for several days on neap tides due to large shoals in the Ouse between Goole and Selby, John Rennie proposed Goole as the highest point on the Ouse to which ships should trade when he reported to the A&CNC in 1818. Accordingly, the company built a new port at Goole and a canal between here and Ferrybridge to allow ready access to and from Leeds, Wakefield and beyond. Many of the scenes pictured in this book owe their origin to the construction of this canal and the rise of Goole as a port. This notice was displayed in 1826 prior to the July opening of the port and canal.

Two

Goole

One of the earliest views of river traffic at Goole is this etching dating from 1830, four years after the port's opening, looking towards Ship Lock, the half-tide basin and the docks, depicting craft including the steam packet *Ebor* in the Ouse. In the days of sail the slow-moving ships preparing to leave the docks were admitted on the level to the half-tide basin. The lock gates were then closed to conserve water in the docks and the level in the half-tide basin lowered. The massed craft then saved time by passing out into the river via Barge Lock or Ship Lock, with the gates of these locks open at both ends, immediately the next tide had produced a sufficient depth of water in the river. Incoming ships could then enter the basin with the tide and wait there before using it as a huge lock to pen up into the docks, thus avoiding possible congestion and grounding in the river. River improvements above Selby in the 1830s allowed *Ebor* to run on a York-Selby-Goole passenger and goods service at any state of the tide, leaving York on Tuesdays, Thursdays and Saturdays and returning from Goole on Mondays, Wednesdays and Fridays.

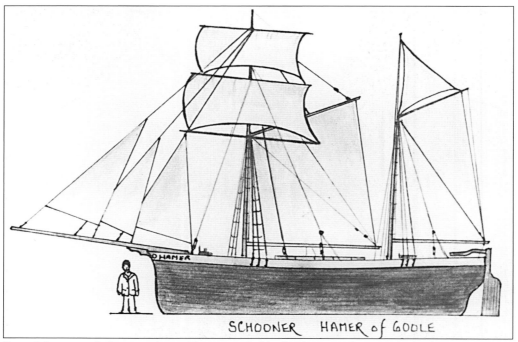

SCHOONER HAMER of GOOLE

Brian Masterman's drawing shows *Hamer*, probably the first vessel ever to be built at Goole and, with approximate dimensions of 37ft x 10ft, one of the smallest sea-going schooners. The vessel was launched in 1826 and built on land adjacent to the canal which became the foundations of the mill used as a vantage point for the photograph on page 37.

The Goole Shipbuiding & Repairing Co. began in 1901 on a site adjacent to the Dutch River, a hastily cut flood relief channel produced in 1633 as an outlet for the River Don into the Ouse. In 1908 they built, as shown, a unique floating hoist, *Alpha*, for tipping coal from compartment boats into ships. At the peak of this, the 'Tom Pudding' system, there were four land-based hoists in addition to this one in the docks contributing to the enormous tonnages of coal exported from Goole. A fuller account is given in Tempus Publishing's *The Aire & Calder Navigation* by Mike Clarke.

During the First World War, the Goole Shipbuilding & Repairing Co. moved their activities onto the Ouse below its confluence with the Dutch River. This aerial view from the 1920s, looking north, shows craft under construction at the new yard with the Dutch River, Barge Lock, Ship Lock and part of the half tide basin visible in the background. *(Masterman Collection)*

This advertisement, featuring the products of the Goole Shipbuilding & Repairing Co., appeared in the A&CNC's handbook published in the late 1930s.

Dredgings from Goole Docks and the nearby canal were responsible for this strange sight in the Ouse off the shipyard. Small A&CNC 'mud boats' were towed out into the river by a Pudding tug and moored whilst their cargoes were shovelled overboard as shown in this photograph from 1936. The practice ended in the late 1950s. *(Masterman Collection)*

One of the more recent vessels to be launched by the former Goole Shipbuilding & Repairing Co. (then Goole Shipbuilders) was the bulk carrier MV *Ballygrainey*, built in 1982 for Kellys of Belfast to carry coal from Garston on the Mersey to Northern Ireland. The vessel is seen here entering the water for the first time with check-wires at the ready. *(Masterman Collection)*

The Dutch River afforded a through route to South Yorkshire for inland waterway craft until Stainforth Lock was closed in 1939. Very few craft venture further than half a mile up the navigation nowadays but here Alan Oliver's narrowboat *Grampus* is shown in 1996 passing under Rawcliffe Bridge to collect used gritsand from another bridge over the river a mile ahead.

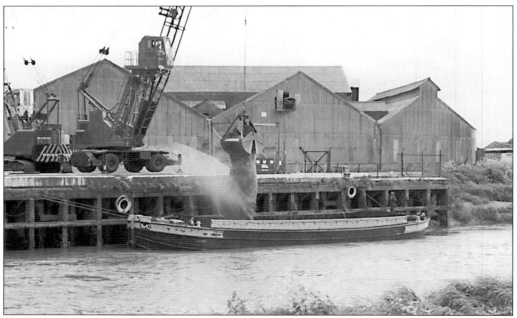

Latter-day traffic on the Dutch River has involved the handling of cargoes at a wharf situated less than a mile above its confluence with the Ouse. Waddingtons' dumb barge *No.40* is shown collecting fluorspar brought in by ship for onward delivery to Rotherham. *(Mike Brown)*

Most shipping comes to the Dutch River Wharf stern-first and the Dutch coaster MV *Vanda* was no exception when it arrived in April 1971 to load 500 tons of fertiliser for Leith. After loading, the vessel began to nose out into mid-river as the early-morning tide came, but the stern remained grounded near the wharf. The fast-flowing water did the rest and *Vanda* was quickly swept athwart the river with its bows sticking on the opposite bank. At low water, the ship was supported only at its bow and stern and there were fears that it could break its back. In the event it merely listed 30° as the cargo shifted and a tug was able to release the vessel undamaged on the evening tide. (*Masterman Collection*)

A much more common type of incident on the Dutch River has tended to occur at the swing bridge crossing it below the wharf and the Antigua-registered MV *Pinnau* became another vessel to experience problems here when coming upriver stern-first in July 1989 with a cargo of potash. The bridge had been swung against road traffic and as the ship approached, the incoming tide swept its bows onto the river's south bank where it grounded as shown with its stern wedged against the bridge's swing mechanism. The tug *Lady Sybil* came from Immingham and pulled *Pinnau* free on the next tide but the road and pedestrian link between Goole and Old Goole had been severed on a Friday night for over twelve hours. (*Masterman Collection*)

A view of tug, barge and ship traffic in the Ouse off Goole dating from pre-1900, taken at about the time of greatest activity close to and before high water. Craft are all pointing downstream for ease of control against the current with a Goole & Hull Steam Towing Co. paddle tug waiting to tow sailing ships out to sea.

A view of river traffic from a similar vantage point to the previous illustration but taken in the 1950s as sea-going craft wait to enter the docks along with two 100-ton capacity tankers belonging to Harkers – the motor barge *Elsie H* and dumb barge *Rosa H* – probably loaded at Saltend with petrol for Leeds. The motor tanker worked up the Ouse to York glassworks on occasions in the 1960s.

Another view of activity in the river off Goole, this time looking downriver in 1935, as T.F. Wood & Co.'s steam towing barge *Ouse* manoeuvres in mid-stream with two of the company's dumb craft *Eleanor* and *Turco Farm* moored close to and above the Ship Lock entrance to the half-tide basin.

Built in 1883 for the Mersey Docks & Harbours Board and purchased by the A&CNC in 1900, the steam-powered *Ouse Tender*, shown here in 1952, worked out of Goole almost daily for over sixty years as a survey and inspection launch on the Lower Ouse between Trent Falls and Hook Swing Bridge. Cylinders of acetylene were delivered to navigation lights, including those at Blacktoft Jetty and Apex Light, before these were converted to electric power. The narrow, tiller-steered vessel was rebuilt during the Second World War, converted to diesel power in 1953 and withdrawn in 1962.

The half-tide basin lies slightly to the left of centre in this aerial view of Goole Docks, dating from the late 1920s, having fallen out of its planned usage after construction of the much larger Victoria Lock had speeded up the movement of craft. It was being used at this time as an assembly point for Tom Puddings waiting to use one of the three tipping hoists visible. The absence of any craft in the locks or river indicates that the photograph was taken outside the period close to high water.

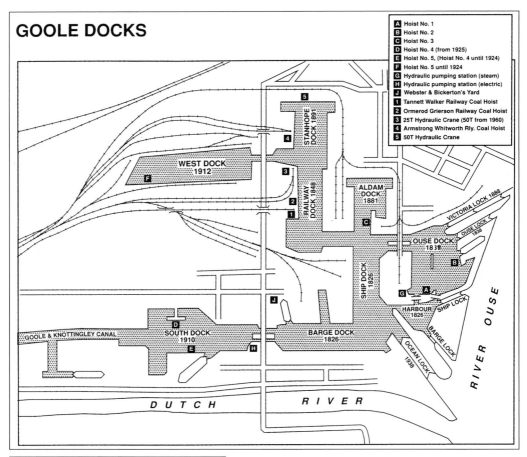

GOOLE DOCKS

A	Hoist No. 1
B	Hoist No. 2
C	Hoist No. 3
D	Hoist No. 4 (from 1925)
E	Hoist No. 5, (Hoist No. 4 until 1924)
F	Hoist No. 5 until 1924
G	Hydraulic pumping station (steam)
H	Hydraulic pumping station (electric)
J	Webster & Bickerton's Yard
1	Tannett Walker Railway Coal Hoist
2	Ormerod Grierson Railway Coal Hoist
3	25T Hydraulic Crane (50T from 1960)
4	Armstrong Whitworth Rly. Coal Hoist
5	50T Hydraulic Crane

STANHOPE DOCK 1891

WEST DOCK 1912

RAILWAY DOCK 1848

ALDAM DOCK 1881

VICTORIA LOCK 1888

OUSE LOCK 1838

OUSE DOCK 1838

SHIP DOCK 1826

HARBOUR 1826

SHIP LOCK

RIVER OUSE

BARGE LOCK

GOOLE & KNOTTINGLEY CANAL

SOUTH DOCK 1910

BARGE DOCK 1826

OCEAN LOCK 1938

D U T C H   R I V E R

Above: A sketch map of Goole Docks, as they were after the opening of Ocean Lock in 1938. The original port of 1826 can be imagined by reference to the dates given. The Harbour (formerly half-tide basin) was filled in and Barge Lock and Ship Lock eliminated in the 1960s.

Left: A wooden sailing keel in Goole's Barge Lock after entering from the Ouse in March 1935. The Piermaster's house is on the extreme left with the lock gatemen's lobby alongside close to the small hand crane used for removing masts and leeboards from craft bound for the A&CN.

Preparations for the opening ceremony at Goole's 360ft x 80ft Ocean Lock in July 1938 are shown with the second SS *Dearne* waiting to enter the lock from the docks. The ship, built for the LMSR in 1924 and becoming part of Associated Humber Lines' fleet on that company's inception in 1935, had been converted to carry refrigerated cargoes on the Goole-Copenhagen service. The vessel was scrapped in 1957.

Ocean Lock in June 1950 as the Ouse Steamship Co.'s SS *Faxfleet* and inland waterway craft pen up into the docks. The company was formed in 1908 and continued to operate until 1961. The 1,100-ton capacity *Faxfleet*, launched in 1916, was the only new vessel ever built for the company and initially served as a fleet collier at Scapa Flow during the First World War before giving thirty-five years of service to its owners, including the Second World War. The vessel was sold for scrap in 1954. (*Masterman Collection*)

A Norwegian barque in the 504ft x 46½ft Victoria Lock at Goole entering or leaving the docks in 1908. The attractive appearance of sailing vessels hardly compensated for their difficulty of handling in the docks where their yards and rigging tended to foul cranes and hoists. (*Masterman Collection*)

Craft using both Victoria Lock and the 264ft x 58ft Ouse Lock in the 1930s. Shipping faced away from the river whether entering or leaving the docks as in both instances control of a vessel was easier when in the Ouse.

A view from atop the mill adjoining Goole's South Dock as James W. Cook & Sons' *Woodcock* C heads through Barge Dock past moored ships and barges in the early 1950s, bound for the A&CN with a cargo of petroleum liquid. A light Tom Pudding steam tug is shown moving in the opposite direction. Ocean Lock, the River Ouse and Dutch River may be seen in the background. South Dock Swing Bridge, in the foreground, was replaced by a more modern structure in 2001. *(Norman Burnitt)*

An advertisement for G.D. Holmes published in the late 1930s as the firm was starting to change over from sailing craft to tugs and motor barges. They traded extensively on all the Humber waterways, including the Ouse, throughout the twentieth century until 1975 by which time all craft had been sold. They also participated in the construction of the Lower Ouse training walls by bringing stone from Barton-on-Humber. Humber keels and sloops are identical apart from their rigging – whereas keels have a single square sail with possibly a topsail, sloops have a mainsail and a foresail and are therefore rigged fore and aft of the mast which is itself stepped further forward than that of a keel. Sloops were generally considered easier to handle than keels and to be more manoeuvrable on estuaries and wide rivers, though interconversion between the two types of sailing craft was possible.

BOCM stored seeds at various waterside depots and here, in August 1979, their motor barge *Selby Margaret* has retrieved some of these from Whitley Bridge and is coming down the A&CN below Pollington Lock en route for Selby via Goole. The photograph was taken from *Marchdale H* which was delivering fuel oil from Immingham to Wakefield.

Cargoes for Selby oil mills were occasionally loaded at Goole as well as Hull and here, in the 1960s, BOCM's *Selby Richard* is shown leaving Goole's West Dock after transhipping about 250 tons of cargo from one of the sea-going vessels moored there. (*Norman Burnitt*)

The iron sloop *Prato*, built in 1927 traded extensively between Goole and York from then until the 1950s, apart from during the Second World War. Each week, about 130 tons of Belgian white sand was collected from one of the railway boats in the docks and the vessel sailed to Selby where it then used the towing service to reach York, before returning to Goole under sail after discharging its cargo at the glassworks. *Prato* is seen here in 1933 waiting to load from SS *Dearne* in West Dock.

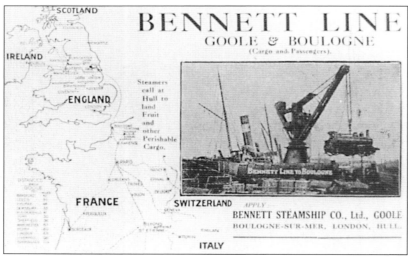

An advertisement dating from the 1920s for the Bennett Line which began its Red Cross Line shipping service from Goole to France in the 1870s, eventually concentrating on Boulogne from the 1880s for the following sixty years. The illustration shows a railway engine destined for Italy being loaded onto their SS *Africa* using the fifty-ton crane in Stanhope Dock. The vessel was lost during the First World War. The company was taken over after the Second World War and its new owners maintained the Goole-Boulogne service for a further twenty-five years.

Ships owned by various other companies were regular visitors to Goole, usually to collect coal, and these are featured on the remaining illustrations in this chapter. Wm France, Fenwick & Co.'s SS *Brenda* is shown, amidst the barge traffic, loading at one of the compartment tipping hoists in Ouse Dock during the 1900s. An accumulator tower, part of the hydraulic system which provided power to work most of the dock apparatus, is visible to the left of the hoist. In 1913, Goole handled 3,900,000 tons of cargo. Of this, 2,775,000 tons were coal with more than 1.5 million tons brought by the puddings and the rest by rail.

Hull Gates Shipping Co.'s MV *Humbergate* built in 1945, is shown loading coal in the 1950s at the hydraulically-powered compartment hoist in South Dock, Goole, with laden Tom Puddings in the foreground. The framework fastened to the hoist was fitted in the 1930s and supported anti-breakage equipment.

Loading of coal ex-railway wagons is shown on these next two illustrations. The 50-ton hydraulic crane in Stanhope Dock is being used in 1957 to lift wagons bodily from the adjacent railway track and tip them into Stephenson Clarke's 1948-built collier MV *Broadhurst*. (*Norman Burnitt*)

Everards' Goole-built MV *Actuality* is shown on this 1957 photograph loading coal from railway wagons brought along an elevated line and tipped at Goole's Tannett Hoist, built in 1906, in Railway Dock. (*Norman Burnitt*)

Three
Goole To Selby

Little changed since its opening in 1869, Hook Swing Bridge, above Goole, shown on this postcard used in 1927, was built by the North Eastern Railway to accommodate the Hull-Doncaster line and carried a double track over the 770ft wide river on its 830ft length. It comprised five 116ft-long fixed spans and a 250ft-long swinging span which pivoted on a central pillar to open a 95ft wide channel on each side. It has been hit by passing craft on many occasions because pilotage on this section of the Ouse has not been compulsory and, despite threats to the contrary, it remains open today still able to be swung in under a minute.

Hook Swing Bridge is shown open for waterway traffic as Lapthorn's MV *Hoo Beech* comes downriver light after delivering a cargo to Selby in February 2001. York City Council were responsible for the Ouse from about twleve miles above York to 200 yards below this bridge until BW took this length over in 1989.

The box-like LASH barges (see page 13) made a welcome reappearance on the Ouse in 1997. This photograph was taken in May 2001 as John Dean's *Freight Endeavour* pushed two barges, each loaded with 380 metric tons of imported rice, upriver beneath Hook Bridge, bound for Selby. Another tug, *Gillian Knight*, had been fastened alongside for extra power to ensure that the voyage was made on one tide. The craft had been brought from the USA to Rotterdam by a mother ship and across to Immingham, where John Dean took over, by a smaller 'feeder' ship.

A rare event in July 2001 as two vessels, travelling in opposite directions, negotiate Hook Swing Bridge simultaneously. MV *Link Trader* is seen passing downstream through the right-hand channel after discharging steel at Howdendyke, whilst the barge *Selby Paradigm* heads upriver to load edible oil at Selby.

In December 1973, a German coaster heading for Howdendyke hit the swinging section of Hook Bridge, bounced across the channel and demolished three of the concrete-filled cast iron pillars whilst knocking one of the fixed spans into the river. Preparations are shown being made to begin repair work in January 1974 but it was ten months before rail traffic could cross the bridge again. The 30ft diameter turntable on which the bridge swings is clearly visible. (*Masterman Collection*)

Fifteen years later, in November 1988, the Swedish freighter MV *Samo* became jammed under one of the bridge's fixed sections after missing the opened section. The ship, bound for Howdendyke with a cargo of packaged timber, claimed to have had a steering failure and was pulled free by three tugs on the next tide. The damage it caused was summarised in British Rail's report as; three spans displaced with No.3 8m out of line at east and 3m at west, two piers damaged and all permanent way rendered unserviceable. British Rail's proposals to close the bridge surfaced again but local government contributed to the cost of repairs enabling it to be reopened.

The Ouse Shipbuilding Co. were established at Hook on the river's west bank in 1917 with 3,000ft of river frontage. Shown in this aerial view are the six building berths capable of holding craft up to 256ft long. The company aimed to complete and launch a new vessel every fourteen days and was a major employer in the area. The yard however, was short-lived, launching its last vessel in 1922 and closing at the end of 1926, having built over eighty vessels if the company's yard numbers can be relied upon to indicate this.

Whitakers' 500-ton capacity *Fusedale* heading down the Ouse in the 1980s after delivering fuel oil to Drax Power Station. Howdendyke wharves may be seen in the background and, on the opposite bank, a water-served oil depot existed from the 1930s to the 1960s, built on part of the former Ouse Shipbuilding Co. site.

The sloop *Sulpho*, owned by Andertons, fertiliser manufacturers of Howdendyke, is shown moored at Stockwith on the Trent in 1906 whilst fully-laden. The company owned a fleet of mostly Howdendyke-built sloops (*Cupro, Hydro, Nitro, Phospho* and *Sulpho*), capable of short sea voyages, which they used between the 1890s and 1930s to import phosphates, pyrites, potash and bone meal, collected from Hull, to their Ouse-side factory. They exported bagged fertiliser in them, along the East Coast, especially to the Wash ports, as well as to local river wharves. (*Humber Keel & Sloop Preservation Society*)

The $61\frac{1}{2}$ft x $15\frac{1}{2}$ft (Sheffield size) steel sailing keel *Sophia* was built at Beverley in 1914, converted to a sloop in 1916 and, when purchased by one of the Barracloughs, renamed *Amy Howson*. Before being motorised and having its rigging removed, the sloop delivered many cargoes to the fertiliser factory at Howdendyke. In 1976, the vessel was purchased by the Humber Keel & Sloop Preservation Society and rerigged as a sloop. *Amy* is seen here in the 1980s under sail off Hull's Fish Dock. (*Les Reid*)

Fertiliser being discharged to lorry from a Russian ship at Howdendyke in 1999 as one of Lapthorn's ships comes downriver from Selby.

The Scarr family established themselves at Howdendyke in 1902, building a boatyard upriver of the village and becoming a limited company in 1934. Before selling out to a company wanting deep water berths in 1968, they built over sixty craft, mainly inland waterway vessels, including *Reklaw*, one of the Ouse's most famous barges. Others will also be seen in this book. This advertisement appeared in the 1950s.

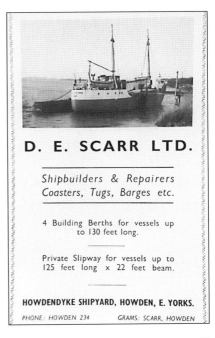

Just above one of the Ouse's most notorious shoals at Clot Hall, near Howdendyke, the M62 bridge was constructed across the river and work on it is shown taking place on this photograph taken in 1974. One year later, the motorway was opened. (*Norman Burnitt*)

Boothferry Bridge was opened in 1929 to replace the last major ferry across the river. A trans-porter bridge was one of the crossings proposed before this 698ft long bridge with a 223ft long swinging span giving a channel width of 125ft was constructed. A steam tug, identified by Lawrie Dews as *Robie*, owned by Selby Oil Mills, is shown heading upriver through the swung span with two barges in tow on this postcard from the 1930s. (*D. Galloway Collection*)

A 1970s view from the motor barge *Selby Michael* as it tows the dumb barge *Selby Cygnus* downriver beneath Boothferry Bridge. The railway-type signal shown on the fixed section was lowered after the opening section had been swung, as is just visible on the previous illustration. In this case there was sufficient headroom beneath the bridge for the craft to pass without any disruption to road traffic. (*Lawrie Dews Collection*)

Taken from the control room atop Boothferry Bridge, *Selby Paradigm* is seen in 2001 heading downriver to Hull with a cargo of rapeseed oil loaded at BOCM Unitrition's recently refurbished Barlby Wharf above Selby. The barge is also shown on page 45 and, before its 1999 installation of tanks, as the graveller *Swinderby* on page 26 of Tempus Publishing's *The River Trent Navigation* by Mike Taylor.

Sloops carrying bricks for York from Broomfleet heading upriver near Boothferry in 1927 at the time when crews slept aboard their craft overnight. These vessels were owned by Williamsons and, in addition to that company, G.D. Holmes, Andertons and James Barraclough & Co. owned and operated fleets of sloops on the Ouse. Barracloughs' *Sprite* was the last one to work under sail, delivering cargoes regularly until 1940 to Scotts' Oil Mill at Selby.

James Barraclough & Co.'s motor barge *A Majestic* passes Boothferry whilst returning light to Hull after delivering a cargo to Selby's Ideal Flour Mill.

In medieval times, the River Aire, another of the Ouse's tributaries, was navigable in favourable conditions upstream to its tidal limit at Knottingley. In the early eighteenth century, locks were constructed along this length at Beal and Chapel Haddlesey to ensure year-round navigation and, by this time, Leeds and Wakefield had also been made accessible by water from Knottingley. After this lock construction, most sea-going craft were unable to reach Knottingley and a trans-shipment centre grew up in the 1740s at Airmyn, near the Aire/Ouse confluence. This was busy until the Selby Canal was opened in 1778, leaving the Aire above Chapel Haddlesey Lock to form a link with the Ouse at Selby which avoided the difficult route to that river via Airmyn and attracted most traffic away from the Lower Aire, though some vessels still used it to avoid paying tolls. In the 1890s, a schooner made what was by then a rare visit to the river and is shown above the 1777-built swing bridge at Snaith. The bridge was replaced in the 1920s. (*Ken Sayner Collection*)

The lock at Chapel Haddlesey was closed in 1937, preventing access to the Lower Aire from above. The river banks still had to be maintained however, and here in April 1998, the motor barge *Daphne* is shown at work stoning the banks at Hirst Courtney, about four miles below the lock site along a tortuous river course.

Stoning the banks of the Lower Aire has been a feature of the river for many years and here, in the 1920s, the sloop *Brilliant Star* lies moored facing upstream at Airmyn loaded with 90 tons of limestone for that purpose. In the 1900s, this vessel, like those owned by Andertons, traded regularly along the east coast between the Humber and ports of the Wash, such as King's Lynn. (*D. Galloway Collection*)

Further up the Ouse at Long Drax, another double track railway swing bridge was opened across the river in 1885 to carry the Hull & Barnsley Railway's line. With a fixed bowstring girder approach span at each side, the 247ft long, centrally pivoted swinging mid-section was operated by hydraulic power generated by a steam engine in the long central pier and gave channels 100ft and 95ft wide. Bridgekeeper Pittaway is seated in the cog boat that he used to scull across river between his house and the steps up to the control cabin atop the swinging section, as two light BOCM craft come downriver in the mid-1950s. The bridge was closed to rail traffic in 1958 and demolished in 1977. *(Charles Pittaway Collection)*

A wharf was specially built close to the Hull & Barnsley Railway's Swing Bridge at Drax to handle the heavy equipment that was shipped there during construction of the the power station, opened in 1968. Subsequently, the wharf was used only spasmodically and, whenever a ship was due to call, the berth had to be dredged. Here, in May 1982, Lincoln & Hull's *Jean Ingelow* is shown removing silt on one of the several occasions it was called upon to do so about that time. *(Lincoln & Hull Marine Contractors)*

Malton from the River.

The River Derwent, another tributary of the Ouse, joins it short distance above the Hull & Barnsley Railway Bridge, at Barmby on the Marsh where a tidal barrage was completed in 1974. Remains of wharves at Malton, thirty-eight miles up the Derwent, where large quantities of coal from West Yorkshire were once discharged, may be seen on this upriver view dating from the 1900s but there has been no regular commercial barge traffic here since the late nineteenth century. The steam launch *Rook* is visible to the left of the photograph.

Bubwith Toll Bridge.

By the start of the twentieth century, railway competition had caused barge traffic on the Derwent to decline. Here, in the 1900s, at Bubwith, the keel *George Sutton* lies moored above the 1798-built toll bridge as *Robert Fox* is poled beneath the navigation arch. Both craft would probably have delivered cargoes to Sutton and now be coming back downriver light. This was a tidal stretch of the river before construction of the barrage at Barmby.

Everards' coastal tanker MV *Aureity heading* up the Ouse to BOCM wharves at Selby in May 1968. (*H.M. Lobley*)

United Towing Co.'s tug *Waterman* hauling Comben Longstaff's bulk carrier MV *Sussexbrook* downriver in February 1970 past Barlow. The ship, recently launched at Cochrane's Selby Yard, would be bound for Goole or Hull to be fitted out. (*H.M. Lobley*)

G.D. Holmes' motor barge *George Dyson* left Goole for Selby on a Tuesday in January 1963 carrying 100 tons of imported bacon to a packing factory. The vessel is shown here trapped in the ice at Roscarrs, $1\frac{1}{2}$ miles short of its destination, having moved up and down the river with the ice surrounding it on several tides. On Friday evening, the barge managed to break free and reach the lowest jetty in Selby outside the sugar factory where its cargo was discharged the following day.

Four

Selby

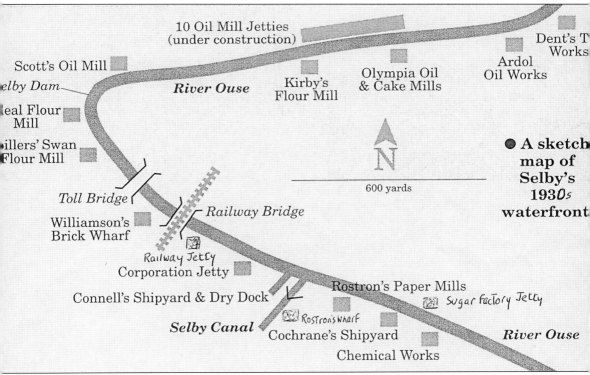

10 Oil Mill Jetties
(under construction)

Dent's T
Works

Scott's Oil Mill

Ardol
Oil Works

elby Dam

River Ouse

Kirby's
Flour Mill

Olympia Oil
& Cake Mills

eal Flour
Mill

illers' Swan
Flour Mill

● A sketch
map of
Selby's
1930s
waterfront

600 yards

Toll Bridge

Railway Bridge

Williamson's
Brick Wharf

Railway Jetty

Corporation Jetty

Rostron's Paper Mills

Connell's Shipyard & Dry Dock

Sugar factory Jetty

Selby Canal

Rostron's Wharf

Cochrane's Shipyard

River Ouse

Chemical Works

Selby was once the busiest port on the Ouse. The tide runs fast through the town along the river's narrow channel and this, together with the two swing bridges sited on a curve, and nearby acute bend have caused many problems for craft. To have control of a vessel moving with the current, it must be travelling faster than that current and, at Selby, this often means moving 'over the ground' at a faster speed than the captain has ever moved on water before. The correct navigational procedure is for a vessel to turn, face the current and move stern-first with engine in forward gear (or in the case of unpowered craft, dragging an anchor), thereby ensuring much greater control over movement. This was often done near the shipyard as a vessel came to Selby on the tide.

Cochranes' Shipyard was a major British shipbuilder and provided employment at Selby from its inception in 1898 to its closure in 1992. Here, in April 1980, MV *Esso Plymouth* is under construction at the yard, two months before its launching. (*Norman Burnitt*)

Rowbothams' tanker MV *Steersman*, lies ready for its 1970 launching at Cochranes' yard as guests assemble for the ceremony. (*Fred Harland*)

Vessels were generally launched broadside into the Ouse with an enormous splash resulting. Here in 1959 the trawler MV *Ross Cheetah* enters water for the first time with local tugs in attendance. *(Fred Harland)*

Cochranes constructed few inland waterway craft but here, the 130-ton capacity tanker barge *Nancy H,* built for Harkers of Knottingley and launched in March 1935, is seen undergoing trials on the Ouse near the yard.

A change of location is to be expected for sea-going craft using the Ouse, but this happens less often for inland waterway vessels. Harkers' *Nancy H*, however, after delivering petrol on the Humber waterways, was transferred to the River Severn to carry the same commodity before being sold in 1959. Here, the barge, now owned by Fox Elms Ltd, is shown leaving Sharpness after conversion to a dry-cargo carrier, bound for Avonmouth to collect a cargo of grain for its owners' Gloucester mill. *(BW)*

Opposite Cochranes on the east bank of the river where a trawler is being fitted out lay the sugar factory's jetty, The motor barges *Reliance* and *Annie H* are shown in the 1960s delivering brown sugar imported from Cuba via Hull. *(Les Hill)*

The Selby Canal joined the Ouse above Cochranes and here, in 1949, on the Calder & Hebble Navigation at Crigglestone in West Yorkshire, Wilby's motor barge *Venture* is loading 80 tons of coal for delivery to York. The vessel would then travel to Wakefield and join the A&CN before passing through Castleford and Knottingley to transit the Selby Canal and finally use the Ouse from Selby to reach its destination.

In the mid-1950s, the motor tanker *Sidney Billbrough* built by Harkers took over collection of coal tar from York's gasworks until the traffic ended a decade later. The vessel is shown during that period preparing to pump off a cargo at Yorkshire Tar Distillers' Knottingley works.

Harkers' 100-ton capacity tanker *Victor H*, fitted with heating apparatus necessary to keep normally viscous liquids mobile, is shown tied up in the 1940s opposite the Anchor pub at Burn Bridge which carries the A19 road across the Selby Canal. The vessel was returning to Yorkshire Tar Distillers at Knottingley with coal tar from York gasworks on the River Foss, having delivered a blended mixture of creosote and pitch to glass manufacturers, also situated on the Foss at York. This was used as a substitute for fuel oil during the Second World War. Apart from this traffic and a little originated by Rowntrees, backloads were notable by their absence on the Ouse, whereas craft delivering to Trent wharves usually returned with gravel and those venturing up the Sheffield & South Yorkshire Navigation or Aire & Calder Navigation brought back coal, making barge movements much more economic on these waterways. *(Ron Gosney Collection)*

A&CNC workmen pose aboard the workboat *Knottingley* in 1958 as they demolish a former LNER bridge over the Selby Canal, near Brayton. (*Ron Gosney Collection*)

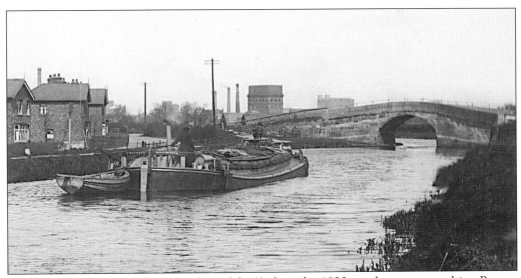

The horse-hauled barge *Kingfisher*, bound for York in the 1920s, is shown approaching Bawtry Road Bridge at Selby with a cargo of West Yorkshire coal. After locking out into the Ouse, one of the City of York's steam tugs would be used to complete the voyage.

The Youth Hostels Association began operating the former grain barge *Sabrina W* as the UK's only floating hostel in 1966. Moored on the canal at Selby and equipped with twenty-one beds, the hostel initially took about 1,500 bed-nights a year despite opening only at Easter, Whitsuntide, July and August. It closed in 1983, having been dogged by vandalism during winter months in its later years. (*William Horn*)

A short arm (Lazy Cut) parallel with and close to the River Ouse, led off the canal at Selby with the river lock nearby. Here, cargoes could be transhipped between ships moored in the river and barges in the cut, thus avoiding the necessity for the latter to go out into the river. Built in the eighteenth century as the canal was opened, it fell into disuse as Goole began to develop after 1826 and, when the small boatyard sited there closed *c.*1900, the stretch of water was closed off and used for the retting of flax (soaking in water to loosen the fibre from the outer part of the plant) to produce linen at a nearby factory. The boatyard is visible on this nineteenth century view, taken looking across the canal into the cut, with laden craft moored next to the lock keeper's house.

With the lock-keeper's house out of shot to the left, James Wilby's motor barge *Surprise* enters the lock at Selby in 1959 carrying a cargo of coal from West Yorkshire bound for York. Originally Wilbys owned only dumb craft but began to change over to motorised vessels in the 1930s. York's Co-op, glassworks, gasworks and a private coalyard were supplied by the company at this time. The changeover to North Sea gas was one of the reasons that the traffic ended in the 1960s.

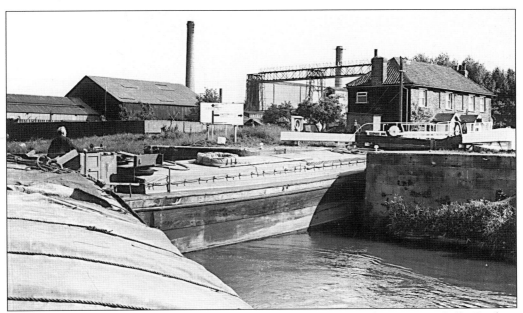

Two unladen barges are shown waiting to enter Selby Canal from the Ouse via Selby Lock in the 1960s. This manoeuvre was often made difficult for a boatman by fast-flowing water in the river. The lock keeper's house seems little changed from the previous century (page 66).

Some idea of the problems caused by the river's fierce flow at Selby may be obtained from this photograph of an incident in 1968. Everards' MV *Aureity* attempted to turn, prior to moving upriver stern-first, by putting its bows into the entrance to Selby Lock. Unfortunately, the coaster became jammed across the river as shown and five inland waterway vessels heading downriver were held up until the next tide.

Holgates' motor barge *Anne M Rishworth* and dumb barge *Florence* after turning head-to-tide whilst coming up the Ouse to Selby light in July 1979.

Just above the entrance lock to Selby Canal, Henry Connell's Boatyard was sited with frontage to the river. Until the late 1950s BOCM had their fleet maintained here. One of the final small pleasure craft to be built at the yard is featured on this double-view, showing the vessel prior to launching using a tractor and then, with mast removed, in the small inlet between the river and the yard. (*Richard Moody Collection*)

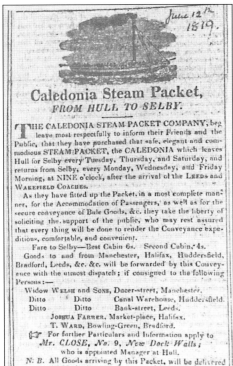

June 12th 1819.

Caledonia Steam Packet,
FROM HULL TO SELBY.

THE CALEDONIA STEAM PACKET COMPANY, beg leave most respectfully to inform their Friends and the Public, that they have purchased that safe, elegant and commodious STEAM PACKET, the CALEDONIA which leaves Hull for Selby every Tuesday, Thursday, and Saturday, and returns from Selby, every Monday, Wednesday, and Friday Morning, at NINE o'clock, after the arrival of the LEEDS and WAKEFIELD COACHES.

As they have fitted up the Packet, in a most complete manner, for the Accommodation of Passengers, as well as for the secure conveyance of Bale Goods, &c. they take the liberty of soliciting the support of the public, who may rest assured that every thing will be done to render the Conveyance expeditious, comfortable, and convenient.

Fare to Selby—Best Cabin 6s. Second Cabin 4s.

Goods to and from Manchester, Halifax, Huddersfield, Bradford, Leeds, &c. &c. will be forwarded by this Conveyence with the utmost dispatch; if consigned to the following Persons :—

Widow WELSH and SONS, Dacer-street, Manchester.
Ditto   Ditto   Canal Warehouse, Huddersfield.
Ditto   Ditto   Bank-street, Leeds.
JOSHUA FARRER, Market-place, Halifax.
T. WARD, Bowling-Green, Bradford.

☞ For further Particulars and Information apply to Mr. CLOSE, No. 9, New Dock Walls; who is appointed Manager at Hull.

N. B. All Goods arriving by this Packet, will be delivered as addressed free of porterage.

A newspaper advertisement dating from 1819 for the Selby-Hull steam Packet service which handled passengers at a jetty on Selby's Ousegate, near to the site of Connell's yard. Another contemporary advertisement featuring an etching of a coach and four horses, related to the *Diligence* coach which delivered passengers to Selby from York and waited the return of the packet from Hull on the day after 'when it immediately sets off for York'.

Lincoln and Hull's crane barges *Mudhook* (left) and *Cité de Paris* working below the railway bridge at Selby in the 1950s on a contract to lay cables beneath the River Ouse. Dumb barges from the oil mills, trailing their anchors to obtain steerage, dropped downriver past this spot to reach Corporation Jetty and wait there for a tow to Hull. Despite warning notices, cross-river cables were occasionally fouled by these trailing anchors. (*Lincoln & Hull Marine Contractors*)

A turn of the century upriver view below the railway bridge at Selby showing sailing vessels on the Ouse and City of York steam tugs moored at the upper of two piers owned by York City Council. (*Richard Moody Collection*)

A downstream view of the original Hull & Selby Railway's 1840-built twin-span cast iron bascule bridge over the Ouse at Selby. The two small lifting sections comprising the left-hand arch were manually operated by means of a quadrant and rack, giving a 64ft wide opening. Despite east coast main line expresses crossing the bridge from 1871, river traffic had right of way over trains. Priorities changed however in 1891 after the original bridge had been replaced and, since then, the three railway swing bridges (Hook, Drax and Selby) have been responsible for most delays to rivercraft. (*Richard Moody Collection*)

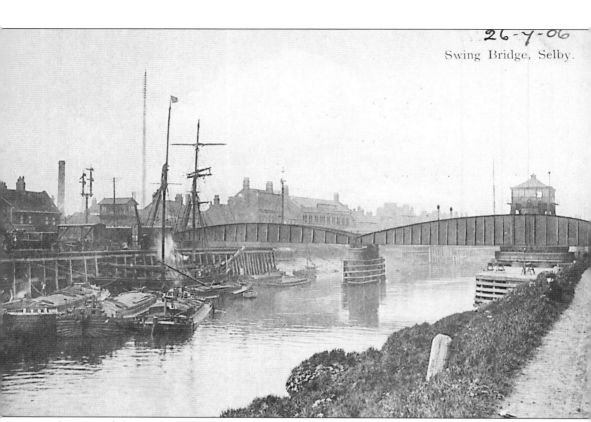

A postcard dating from the 1900s of the 1891-built replacement railway bridge built slightly downstream of the original, showing the 129ft long, hydraulically-operated swinging span and the 111ft fixed span, with craft moored at the adjacent Railway Jetty. A tow of four barges coming upriver would have been rearranged from V-formation into single file outside the chemical works by the mate of the first barge on the port side of the V hauling in its 120ft long, 10in diameter tow rope before handing it across to the second barge on the starboard side of the V to be reconnected. Barely visible are the 'spectacles' on the fixed span which dropped to indicate that the bridge was open for shipping. Should the skipper of a tug towing a train of barges upriver on a big tide find the spectacles unmoved after giving one long and six short blasts, the whole single file tow would have to be turned 'head to tide' outside the shipyard to halt forward movement. When the signal that the bridge was opening was subsequently seen, the tow would be turned again and the tug given full power to ensure steerage through the bridge for itself and its barges. After several accidents when craft coming upriver were given the 'spectacles' to pass the railway bridge only to be confronted by a closed toll bridge as they rounded the curve, the spectacles were used to indicate the opening of both bridges. Only since the early 1980s has radio contact between bridges and vessels been established. The east coast main line was rerouted away from here in 1983.

A view from almost the same angle as the previous one as Acasters' *Kirkby* heads upriver through the swung railway bridge in January 1984 with 85 tons of paper, bound for York. The control cabin atop the swinging section had been raised in anticipation of the installation of overhead power lines for the electrified main line, but these were never fitted.

Two former Ouse-based craft now owned by Acasters are featured in this photograph taken in 1999. *Selby Libra*, one of the final two dumb vessels to be built for BOCM's Selby mills, and *Little Kirkby*, converted to a push tug by shortening the barge pictured above, are shown leaving Goole with a cargo of fluorspar for Rotherham on the S&SYN. *Kirkby has* had a strange history since being built in 1959 to Sheffield size by Camplings of Goole. It was lengthened by 42ft before being purchased by the present owners who shortened it by 18ft to pass readily through York's Castle Mills Lock. Finally the barge was further shortened by 32ft to produce *Little Kirkby*. (*Mike Brown*)

Another Selby 'incident' is featured on this downriver view as the Dutch coaster MV *Heljo*, bringing 500 tons of grain to Ideal Mill, lies stuck across the river, jamming the railway swing bridge open, thus closing the main London-Edinburgh line for about eight hours in March 1967. Lawrie Dews who spent a lifetime aboard the BOCM fleet working to/from Selby is fully aware of the problems both here and at the Toll Bridge when craft come upriver shortly after high water against the current. As the vessel passes into the bridgehole, the river is effectively dammed and, if it then ceases to make headway against the force of the current, the only remedy is to fall back and try again. Some craft however, keep trying with their engines full ahead, the bows are pushed off-course by the current sweeping around the slight bend in the river and the ship or barge is unable to counter this because its position beneath the bridge prevents the usual steering movements of its stern. The fore end of the vessel is then usually forced against the bank and held there by the current before, if lucky, it can be pulled free twelve hours later on the next tide. (*H.M. Lobley*)

The road and rail bridges, 180 yards apart, across the Ouse at Selby looking downstream from the top of Ideal Mill in December 1983. A coaster lies moored at the wharf between the bridges, one further away beyond the rail bridge is on the move close to the entrance to Selby Canal, and a third ship is being fitted out at Cochranes in the distance.

This inaccurate representation of an upriver view of Selby Toll Bridge appeared on a postcard published in the 1920s. The etching, dating from 1830, depicts the 1792-built bridge having too many piers that are wrongly positioned crossing an excessively wide river with a swinging section opening to produce two channels instead of one. The rowing boats would be most unlikely to be found on such a fast flowing river and anyway all such craft apart from those used by salmon fishermen were sculled with a single oar at the stern. The use by historians of such pictures for factual evidence is unwise.

This photograph of the City of York steam tug *Ebor Express* heading downriver through Selby Toll Bridge provides a much more accurate record of the structure. The narrow passage adjacent and to the left of the opened section was never used for navigation but, in an emergency, craft could perhaps squeeze under the wider fixed arch immediately to the left of this.

The oil mills' steam tug *Robie* heading upstream in the 1920s past Selby Toll Bridge with towline taut, indicating barges under tow, probably bound for the crushing mill wharves at Barlby.

Selby Warehousing & Transport Co. was set up as the oil mills' transport subsidiary shortly after the First World War. This letterhead is taken from a communication with York City Council dealing with the sale of steam tug *Robie* to the Selby company in 1920.

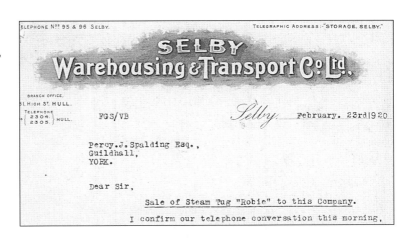

The wooden toll bridge was replaced by a steel structure in 1970, though tolls were not abolished until 1991. With the tide flowing upriver, Whitakers' *Blackbird*, bound for York glass-works in August 1983 with a cargo of fuel oil from Immingham, obeys the Ouse Navigation's bye-law No.14 which states: 'No master of a vessel shall pass Selby Toll Bridge except (i) at slack water or against the stream, or (ii) going astern with the stream.' This photograph of the tanker barge obeying (ii) and heading upriver with the flood tide was taken from the railway swing bridge. As a matter of pride, some reckless old-time tug skippers tended to ignore this ruling and 'ran the bridges', towing their barges through with the current at some risk, but thereby avoiding the delay caused by rounding up to drop the barges through. *Blackbird* made the final delivery of oil to the glassworks in December 1983.

Along with Hook Railway Swing Bridge, Selby Toll Bridge has been the scene of many accidents on the Ouse, several caused by the situation described on page 77. This report dating from 1917 describes an encounter between two trains of barges. Verbal accounts of incidents later in the twentieth century have reported suspicions from radio communications of drunkenness aboard the ships involved.

Most of the accidents at Selby Toll Bridge tended to cause considerable inconvenience by closing access to the town for pedestrians and traffic coming from York and the east. In May 1930, Everards' coaster MV *Agility*, coming upriver to the Olympia Oil & Cake Mills' wharves, jammed its bow beneath the swing section of the toll bridge. The rising tide then caused the vessel to lift this section off its bearings and deposit it into the river as shown. Also visible to the left of the illustration is the emergency cross-river ferry service provided by owners of the Toll Bridge which operated until the bridge was reopened after repair, six weeks later. (*Richard Moody Collection*)

The coaster MV *Valery* appears to be making a smooth passage at the new Selby Toll Bridge in May 1981 but, in reality, is slightly off course and stuck between the piers with the opening section jammed in position against road and footpath traffic. A more unusual incident at the toll bridge happened in July 1985 when, attempting to replicate an invasion of York which took place more than 1,000 years earlier, a group of Norwegian boat enthusiasts set off up the Ouse towing the small, 150-year-old Viking longboat *Rissa*, apparently unaware that Selby Toll Bridge had been built in the meantime. They arrived at Selby running with a strong tide and failed to round up. The towing vessel passed through the bridge's navigation channel, but *Rissa* hit a bridge pier and headed beneath one of the fixed spans. As the towrope became taut, the longboat was dashed to pieces against the pier. Despite a representative of Yorvik Viking Centre at York claiming that 'There is no way that it will be left in the Ouse', the strong currents in the river ensured that only a 1ft length of the vessel was ever found.

Initially, the oil mills' fleet of dumb barges was towed by their own steam tug *Robie* augmented by those of York City Council and Whitakers' *Cawood* and *Wilberforce*. With *Robie* now ready for scrapping and the sale of York's *Lancelot* imminent, OCO and *Ardol*, two TID tugs built during the Second World War, were purchased in 1947. Here OCO is hauling *Selby Virgo* away from the Toll Bridge after it had gone athwart of the structure whilst dropping downriver to the Corporation Jetty to wait for a tow to Hull. *(Fred Harland)*

During the 1920s, after successfully negotiating Selby Toll Bridge, the steam tug *Robie* hauls its tow of barges upstream in single file towards the acute bend in the river and the oil mill wharves beyond.

Missing from the previous photograph is the Ideal Flour Mill, opened in 1933 situated on the outside of an acute bend in the river. A German coaster is shown discharging at the mill in January 1980. Prior to Rotterdam's takeover of Hull's position as the major European port in the 1960s, motor barges owned by James Barraclough & Co. delivered all the mill's grain from Hull and coasters did not come to this wharf. (*Norman Burnitt*)

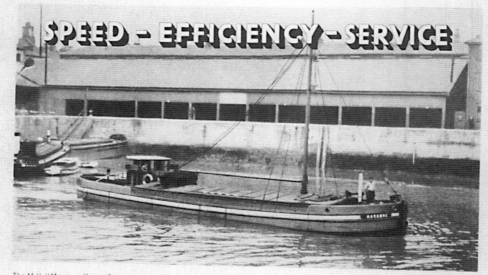
A Barraclough advertisement published in the A&CNC's brochure of the late 1930s. The motor barge illustrated, *Maranne*, made many voyages to the Ideal Flour Mill.

Five
Selby to York

An aerial view, looking upstream, of the wharves at Barlby dating from the 1930s. Kirbys' Flour Mill and its wharf where two craft lie moored are situated close to the camera whilst most other wharves belong to the oil mills. All cargoes had to be taken across the road running close to the mills by various means. Railway access to the oil mills was also provided from the East Coast main line seen passing the mills on the opposite side from the river.

A 1930s view from the Ouse's right bank showing part of the oil mills' fleet of thirty-five 200-ton capacity dumb barges, some of which were built at Scarrs of Howdendyke. Four of these craft were able to carry either liquid or solid cargoes. From left to right along the riverfront lie one of the three bucket elevators, the oil wharf with canisters visible, the Telfer and Kirbys' Mill.

The oil mills' Telfer, a 1910-built engineering wonder, discharging bagged cargo from a by-trader's barge in the 1950s.

In the early 1950s, BOCM decided to dispense with their fleet of dumb barges and replace them with eighteen new motor barges which were to be built between 1952 and 1963 by Dunstons of Thorne. This is the September 1962 launching picture of their 250-ton capacity *Selby Margaret*. (*Norman Burnitt*)

Selby Michael, another of the motor barges built at Dunstons which was launched in 1960, is seen leaving the BOCM wharves at Barlby to fight its way downriver through the ice in January 1963. The company ceased to carry by barge in 1982 and used them for storage purposes until the 1990s when they were sold.

The 200-ton capacity *Selby Ellen*, one of the earliest motor barges to be built by Dunstons for BOCM, is shown in 1999 after its sale and subsequent refurbishment on the A&CN at the confluence of the Rivers Aire and Calder outside Castleford, bound for Leeds with a cargo of Trent aggregate. *(Mike Brown)*

The Dutch-built coaster MV *Freda W* is shown in 1984 discharging a 600-ton cargo of seeds at BOCM's suction elevators near their oil mills, using *Selby Argo*, a member of the company's former dumb barge fleet, as a mooring pontoon. Crescent Shipping's 500-ton capacity coaster MV *Blatence* lies moored further upriver at the Ardol jetty. The Ardol Co. was formed in the First World War to hydrogenate oils.

Grain being discharged from a lighter at BOCM's Barlby Wharf in August 1981 by a suction elevator assisted by a 'Bobcat'. (*Sheila Nix Collection*)

Most former boatmen who worked on the Ouse can be relied upon to identify the site of a picture with pinpoint accuracy. However, this clinker-built keel (see pages 38 and 52 for comparison with a sloop) with sail half-raised is coming down the Ouse at a location which leaves them unsure, perhaps due to the absence of distinctive features in the picture. Lawrie Dews and Jim Barley thought it could be on the straight above BOCM's Barlby oil mills, Dick Cressey plumped for No Man's Friend, below Selby and Les Hill independently suggested that it could be at either one of these locations.

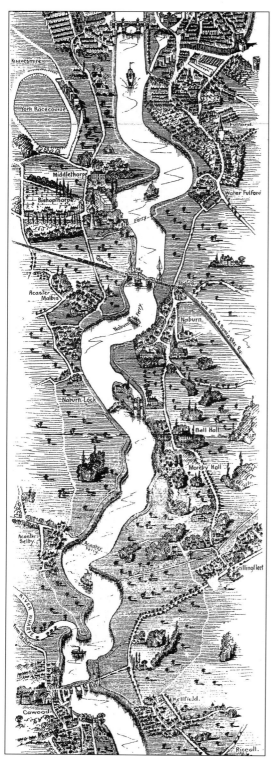

Another part of the 1891 bird's-eye view of the Ouse. The stretch between Cawood and the Ouse/Foss confluence in York is featured. (*Courtesy of the* Yorkshire Post)

Woods' steam towing barge *Ouse* heading upriver through Cawood in the 1940s with a loaded dumb barge in tow almost certainly bound for the former Leethams' Warehouse on York's River Foss, then owned by Rowntrees the chocolate manufacturers. Built for the company in 1890 by Watsons of Gainsborough, the vessel's funnel was readily lowered, often allowing it to save time at swing bridges without needing to wait for them to be moved. *Ouse* was disposed of in 1957. (*Andrew Bryce Collection*)

The road swing bridge at Cawood replaced a ferry across the river in 1872 and a dumb vessel is shown moving upriver stern-first through the structure in the 1920s. An anchor is being trailed from its bows to give steerage and one of the crew has a stower to hand ready to push off from the bridge pier, if necessary.

Eastwoods' motor barge *Brilliant Star*, shown on page 54 as a sailing sloop, approaching Cawood Swing Bridge in the early 1970s bound for York. The vessel was fitted with a diesel engine in 1933 and lengthened by 25ft in 1971, to improve its carrying capacity. *(Les Reid)*

Coal being unloaded *c.*1900 from the keel *Britannia* moored at the Old Crane Wharf on the River Wharfe below the bridge at Tadcaster. The child seated on the furled sail on which the barrow run also rests, as well as the poses taken by all the men shown, indicate that the photographer's visit was considered an important event. Barge traffic at Tadcaster gradually declined in the twentieth century. A sand barge, owned by a local builder, was the last vessel to work here, dredging its cargoes from the river bed. It ceased work in the late 1940s.

The weir and lock at Naburn, built in 1757, then made this point the tidal limit of the Ouse which was previously above York, Faced with diminishing traffic to the city caused by tran-shipment of York-bound cargoes from sea-going vessels to craft small enough to pass through the original (90ft x 21½ft) lock, York City Council built a larger lock (150ft x 26ft) alongside the older one in 1888. The weir and both locks are shown from the river's west bank on these two upriver postcards dating from the 1900s.

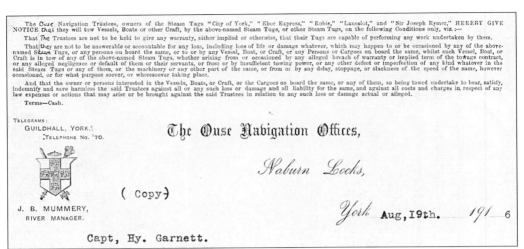

York City Council's Ouse Navigation offices were sited at Naburn locks and conditions for towing by their steam tugs were set out on their letter headings as shown here. In 1818, twelve schooners traded via the old lock between York and London. 1905 was the Ouse's busiest year above Naburn with more than 373,000 tons of cargo passing on the river, five sixths of which involved Henry Leetham & Sons' mill on the River Foss at York. In this year, the Derwent carried only 6,076 tons up to Sutton and the Ure Navigation, above York, 3,409 tons.

Whitakers' tanker barge *Jondor*, waiting to pen up through Naburn lock in October 1978 with a cargo of fuel oil for York glassworks. This vessel made at least one delivery per week to the glassworks between the mid-1950s and 1980.

Woods' *Bustardthorpe* heading for the larger lock at Naburn in the 1960s, loaded with 120 tons of cocoa beans for Rowntrees., having successfully negotiated shoals at Wharfe Mouth, Acaster Selby and Mawby Hall which often built up in the summer months before being partially washed away by autumn rains. Several vessels have run aground on the latter shoal as spring tides were falling off and been neaped there for a week. *(Pete Hunsley)*

Chris Oatway is shown on this October 1978 photograph raising the gate paddle of the large lock at Naburn to pen down his ex-BW motor barge *Lambda*. The vessel was bound for a River Trent gravel wharf to load another cargo for York. *Lambda* has since been converted to a land-based pub in Leeds.

Acasters' diesel push-tug *Little Shifta* is shown in 1994 at Naburn with its two barges, loaded with paper, setting off along the lock cut bound for the Evening Press Wharf on the River Foss at York. The craft had just been reconnected after passing up through the locks. The barges penned through the large lock whilst the tug used the smaller 1757-built lock. Woods' *Ouse* and the two barges it was towing penned through here in similar fashion nearly a century earlier, the major difference being that *Ouse* pull-towed its barges.

Motor barge *Fossgate* and dumb barge *Lowgate*, owned by the Anglo-American Oil Co. (later to become Esso) are shown unladen above Naburn Locks in the 1930s, waiting to pen down after delivering petrol to York.

A hold-up in Naburn Cut in the 1930s with coal barges, a steam tug/barge and Woods' *Belle Alliance* amongst craft detained possibly by low water levels as work on the weir took place. T.F. Wood served in France during the First World War and took refuge at *Turco Farm* for a time, November 1918 being a *Belle Alliance*. The names given to the two 125ft long ex-Belgian members of his company's fleet commemorated this. Their length made them unable to work to Foss wharves above Castle Mills Lock

Leeds Magnetic, once a member of BOCM's fleet of dumb barges but now motorised, is shown heading out of Naburn Lock Cut in 1986 with a cargo of Trent aggregate bound for Clifton, above York, where a new bridge was being constructed to carry a by-pass around the city.

On river navigations such as those based on the Don, Ouse and Trent, the river itself flows over a weir whilst craft pass using a lock and lock cut. Occasionally, in times of flood, boatmen chose to ignore the lock and come over the weir. Here, in January 1962 with river levels normal, Woods' motor barge *Ouse* is stuck on the weir because vandals deliberately cast the vessel adrift from its moorings in York and it came downstream with the current. A crane barge is being used to transfer the 100-ton cargo to another vessel below the weir before *Ouse* can be pulled free. This *Ouse* was acquired by Woods after they had sold their steam towing barge of the same name (shown on pages 32 and 88).

Six

York's River Foss

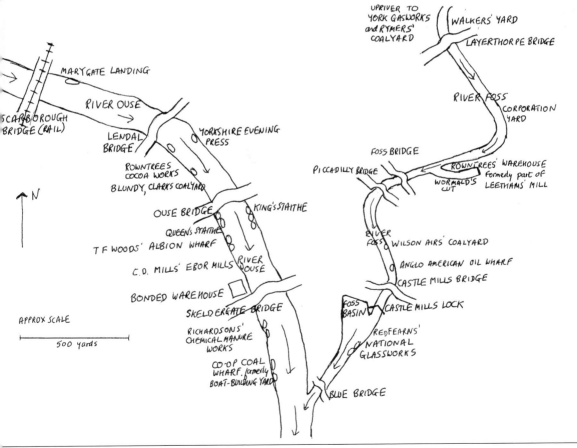

A sketch map of York's wharves in the late 1930s provided by the late R.W. Cowl.

A drawing of the Foss/Ouse confluence below York, dating from 1703 when both rivers were tidal.

BLUE BRIDGE, YORK.

A postcard of the Foss/Ouse confluence in the 1900s showing the manually operated lifting footbridge over the former and many vessels moored below Skeldergate Bridge on the west bank of the latter. The original 1738-built wooden drawbridge on the site was painted blue.

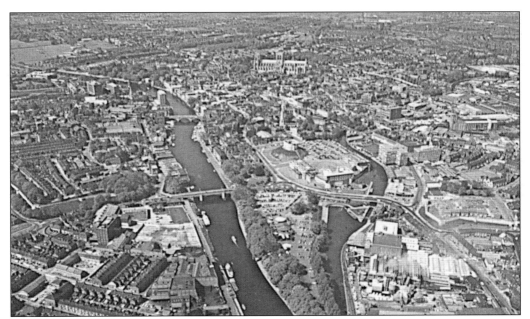

An aerial view of York in the 1950s showing the Ouse (left) and Foss. Castle Mills Lock and the glassworks with its attendant polluting smoke are visible (lower right).

The dumb barge *Mary*, built in 1910 by Watsons of Gainsborough for Sir Joseph Rymer, was used to bring coal from West Yorkshire to the city. The vessel is moored outside York glassworks on the Foss, close to its confluence with the Ouse. Its Captain, Mr T. Whitton, stands posed at the bow and his family at the stern. (*Jarvis Whitton Collection*)

The crew of Whitakers' *Marchdale* connecting pipes prior to discharging 200 tons of fuel oil shortly after arrival at York's glassworks in July 1980. The glassworks' weekly order occasionally had to be delivered over three voyages instead of one during low summer river levels, with cargoes as small as 70 tons being brought on occasions. The traffic ended in 1983 after over fifty years.

An early twentieth century postcard view of Castle Mills Lock and Bridge looking towards York's Castle and Clifford's Tower with craft moored in Foss Basin, off the Ouse. (*Hugh Murray Collection*)

Castle Mills Lock on York's River Foss drained for repairs in June 1922 with intermediate gates visible together with pointed sills for the bottom gates. (*Hugh Murray Collection*)

Acasters' push tug *Little Shuva* bringing the lighter *Twite* through Castle Mills Lock in February 1997, bound for the *Evening Press* premises. This traffic was York's final involvement with commercial carrying by inland waterway and finished two months later.

In August 1982, Holgates' *Anne M Rishworth* brought 120 tons of cocoa beans to York for discharge at Rowntrees' Wharf on the River Foss. Unfortunately the barge and Castle Mills Lock were of approximately the same length and, though it had passed through the lock many times previously, the bottom gates could not be closed this time. Wood was shaved from the lock gates and the vessel spent several hours trying to squeeze in with its engine at 'full ahead' as shown until, after almost twenty-four hours, the bottom gates could be closed and the barge penned up to continue its voyage for the short distance remaining.

T.F. Wood & Co.'s new Beverley-built motor barge *Brunton* undergoing trials on the Humber in January 1934.

<u>Notes on Brunton's Accident at Castle Mills Lock, York</u>

River Engineer
On the morning of 20th May 1958, the *m.v.Brunton* crashed into the lower lock gates at Castle Mills Lock when they were closed and, in so doing, ripped the west side gate off its hinges and deposited it in the lock bottom. This incident caused the top gates to become badly buckled and allowed the waters of the River Foss to drain away.

Dick Cressey, *Brunton's* Captain
I blew for the lock to be turned around as I approached but the lockkeeper was nowhere in sight so I went to the lock tail to put my mate ashore to do the job. I put the engine to 'Astern' but it stalled The boat carried on moving forward, bounced off the wall and hit the right-hand gate which partly opened. The left-hand gate sprung outwards and broke away with the force of water which was great because the top gates of the lock had been left open. We were carried backwards on a huge wave and the Foss was drained.

Counsel's Report
Accepted the fact that a prototype engine was fitted at the time and that tests had shown that it tended to stall when put astern from ahead. Counsel was of the opinion that there was no point in taking action against the skipper of *Brunton* since he would probably prove to be a man of straw.

Final Outcome
The lock was closed for a period of 9 weeks for repairs. Claims by companies using the Foss, including Rowntrees, Walkers and the Gas Board, were allowed, together with York's costs of effecting repairs, in the Admiralty Division of the High Court of Justice in London.

A downstream view of the River Foss drained for maintenance above Castle Mills Bridge in June 1904. *Brunton's encounter with the nearby lock in 1958 produced a similar scene. (Hugh Murray Collection)*

An early photograph of Henry Leetham & Sons' Mill, established in 1850, on the west bank of the Foss in York's Hungate. The mill was connected by a bridge across the river to their 1889-built warehouse on Foss Island which lay between the Foss and Wormald's Cut. The river was also improved at the same time by ensuring that it had a $7\frac{1}{2}$ft depth up to here. Until their preferential toll rates were withdrawn in 1924, Leethams were responsible for most of York's inland waterway traffic.

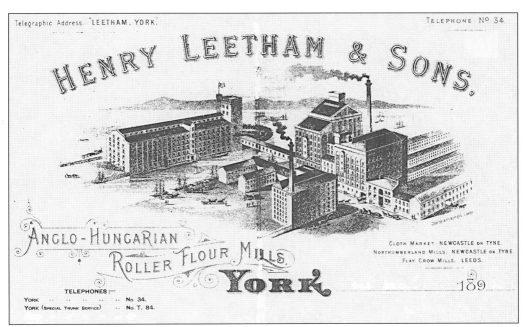

A Henry Leetham & Sons letter heading from the 1890s featuring an etching of an aerial view loosely based on the company's York premises showing the two sites connected by a bridge across the Foss. The river however, seems excessively wide and the apparent close proximity of the sea owes little to reality.

Leethams ceased to bring cargoes to their warehouse in 1930 and it was sold to Rowntrees in 1934. Woods' dumb barge *Cecil* is shown in 1973 moored on the Foss whilst discharging a bagged cargo at the warehouse. (*Sheila Nix Collection*)

Woods' *Bustardthorpe*, built as a dumb barge by Watsons at Gainsborough in 1914 and motorised in 1931, is shown discharging a bagged cargo on the Wormald's Cut side of Rowntrees' warehouse in the 1950s. An occasional backload of cocoa residues was loaded here for Hull.

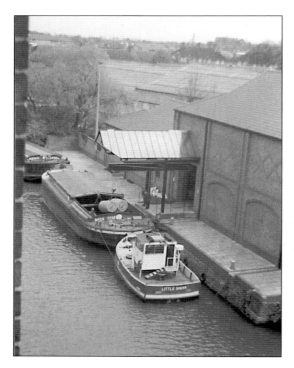

In the 1990s, Rowntrees' Warehouse was sold and converted into flats. The *York Evening Press* moved their operation from the Ouse to purpose-built premises on Wormald's Cut and this photograph, taken from one of the flats, shows reels of paper being discharged from Acasters' barge *River Star* at the newly-built newspaper wharf with the tug *Little Shuva* in attendance. *(Mike Brown)*

Girls fishing from Corporation Wharf in July 1971 as craft discharge at Rowntrees' Navigation Warehouse lower down the Foss. (*Sheila Nix Collection*)

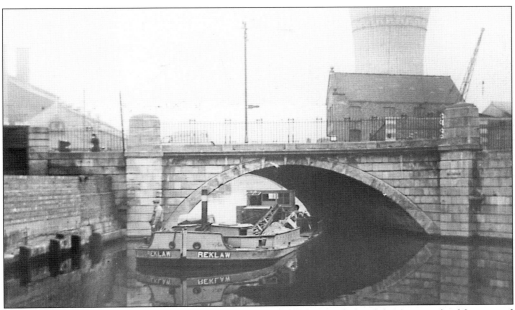

J.H. Walker & Co. had *Reklaw* built in 1925 by Scarrs of Howdendyke to win building sand from the beds of local rivers. It was a familiar sight in York for over fifty years and is shown here passing beneath Layerthorpe Bridge in the 1960s to bring another cargo of sand to its owners' wharf, a few yards ahead. Walkers moved their operation a short distance downriver to Corporation Wharf in 1973.

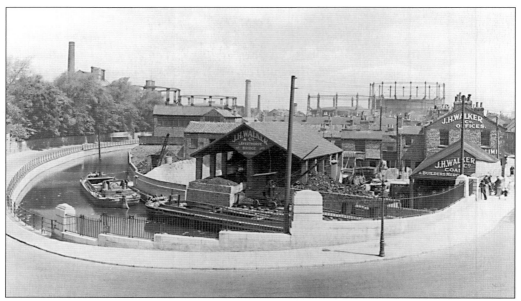

This 1920s publicity photograph used by Walkers shows their Layerthorpe Yard on York's River Foss. The motor barge *Reklaw* may be seen in its original form on the left with an open wheelhouse and mast and derrick for use in winning sand from the river bed using a canvas bag fitted with a steel cutting edge. The Priestman dredging crane shown on the previous photograph was fitted to replace this in 1947, reducing the barge's cargo-carrying capacity from around 100 tons to 50 tons. A new covered wheelhouse was fitted a couple of years later, by which time the crew had almost finished sleeping aboard overnight. (*Bill Harris Collection*)

A downriver view of empty coal barges moored on the Foss outside York gasworks, built in the late nineteenth century close to the railway siding which also carried coal to the premises. Coal deliveries by barge of over 1,000 tons per week developed after the Second World War and ended *c.*1960.

Harkers' tanker *Lincoln*, built as a steam barge in 1903 by Watsons of Gainsborough, was converted to diesel power in the 1930s. From the early 1930s, the vessel began collecting tar from York gasworks for delivery to Yorkshire Tar Distillers at Knottingley and, during the Second World War, participated in the loaded-both-ways traffic described on page 64. Unlike *Victor H* however, *Lincoln* was not fitted with cargo-heating coils and had to load the liquids when they were hot, aimimg then to complete the voyage and pump off before the cargo became too viscous. The tanker, which was scrapped in 1956, is shown here at work in the 1940s.

This picture, dating from the 1900s, was taken looking downstream on the River Foss from Rymer Bros' coalyard at Monk Bridge. An accident victim seems to have been placed on a stretcher near to the clinker-built keel with sail furled. (*Hugh Murray Collection*)

OUSE NAVIGATION

TOWING LICENCES ISSUED AND RENEWED FOR YEAR ENDING 31ST DECEMBER, 1949.

Owner.	Name of Tug	Master
Anglo-American Oil Co. Ltd.	Fossgate Tetney	William Campbell Joe Sayner
James Wilby Ltd.	Venture Stedfast Reliance Rex Nox Intrepid	Laurence Tomlinson Cuthbert Sykes Herbert Haigh Ernest Waller G.W.Lovell Ben Johnson
James Barraclough and Co. Ltd.	Maranne A. Majestic A. Victory Juneville A. Triumph	Norman W. Barraclough George Edward Fisher Richard Richardson Reginald R. Barraclough Harold Harness
Blundy Clark and Co. Ltd.	Etheredge Henrietta Clark Catherine Clark Doris Clark	Samuel Hall William Kirby Thomas Hobson Thomas Walker
Olympia Oil and Cake Co. Ltd.	Robie Oco	Thomas Hall Berrick Thomas Greaves
T.F. Wood and Co.Ltd.	Ouse Brunton Bustardthorpe Bishopthorpe	(Frederick Bucknell (Alfred Edward Cawthorne (George Wm. Jefferson (Max Rook - Robert Bowyer Cressey
Cristo Ltd.	John M. Rishworth Rose	Harold West Gardiner Richard Arthur Bower
United Towing Co. Ltd.	Seeker	Thomas Legarde Maddra
Goole and Hull Steam Towing Co. Ltd.	Salvage	E. Richardson
G.D. Holmes Ltd.	Vista Hiddekel Fremantle	Wilfred Barley James Barley Clarence Shirtliff.
John Harker Ltd.	Lion H.	J.W. Addinall

NOTES:- (i) T.F. Wood and Co. Ltd. - Masters' licences issued in respect of tug named and other tugs owned by T.F. Wood and Co. Ltd.

(ii) Fee of £1. 1. 0d. received in respect of each licence issued and paid over to City Treasurer.

A list of motor barges which worked up to York in 1949, often towing dumb craft belonging to their owners, is given in this record of towing licences issued by York City Council.

Seven
York and the Ouse

Returning to the Ouse, two wooden keels are shown lying outside Clementhorpe Shipyard below Skeldergate Bridge in the late nineteenth century when it was owned by Connells who also had a yard at Selby (see page 69). The inner one is clinker-built (overlapping planks), whilst a workman standing on a small punt is attending to the outer vessel. Replacing a ferry, Skeldergate Bridge was opened as a toll bridge in 1881 with tolls abolished in 1894. Passage of fixed-masted craft was effected through the small right-hand arch where two ornamental sections on each side of it swung outwards before the carriageway was lifted. The boatyard was closed in 1935, the towpath bridge and slipway being filled in shortly afterwards.

A posed photograph dating from 1909 shortly after York Equitable Industrial Society had built a bacon factory, bakery and coal depot alongside the Ouse next to the boatyard. Craft lie moored on the river and several horse and dray pairs stand on the wharfside. (*Hugh Murray Collection*)

The Cooperative Society built a wharf fitted with a gantry-mounted Telfer style grab on the former site of the boatyard after it fell into disuse. Here, Wilby's *Stedfast* and *Rapidity* are shown at the wharf in the mid-1950s, their cargoes of West Yorkshire coal being discharged as a trip boat heads downriver. This wharf too fell into disuse in the 1960s. (*Bill Harris Collection*)

A workman kneeling at the end of a long plank attends to *Enterprize* below Skeldergate Bridge as the steam tug *Lancelot* turns after casting off the vessel, visible through the arch, that it had brought upriver. The tug's fixed funnel would have needed the navigation arch of the bridge to be swung had it travelled further upriver. *(Vic Dickenson Collection)*

With *Prato* and *Hydromel* the only dumb craft then using their towing service (to bring sand from Goole to York's glassworks), York City Council ended their towing service in 1947 and sold *Lancelot*, their sole remaining tug, to Peter Foster & Co. of Hull. The vessel is seen here in 1959 along with *Acetut*, another member of the Foster fleet, bringing the newly built Spurn lightship down the River Hull from its Beverley builders. The lightship remained neaped in this position for several days. *(D. Grindell Collection)*

A postcard view taken from Skeldergate Bridge, with Ouse Bridge and several west bank wharves visible in the background, as the pleasure cruiser *River King* heads downriver past the Bonded Warehouse. From its introduction in 1901 to its replacement in 1932, *River King* cruised up to Clifton and down to Bishopthorpe between Easter and September each year. This non-tidal stretch of the Ouse has been the scene of leisure activities on the river for many years.

Illustrated on a postcard used in 1905 is the transfer of a barge's bagged cargo, using the vessel's mast and derrick, to a horse-drawn dray on the west bank of the Ouse above Skeldergate Bridge.

C.D. Mills & Co.'s Ebor Mills, on the Ouse's west bank between Skeldergate and Ouse bridges, were severely damaged by fire in April 1911 and here, the City of York steam tug *Sir Joseph Rymer* is shown attempting to dampen down the premises after the blaze. The company continued to operate until the 1930s. The tug's steam engine and boiler were fitted to Woods' *Ouse* after *Sir Joseph Rymer* was withdrawn from service in 1937.

Taken from approximately the same position on the east bank as the previous photograph but before the fire, this downriver view shows the Ouse in 1910, at a time when Naburn Weir was not damming the water flowing through York, probably due to maintenance work taking place with the sluices raised. The low water level would not have been regularly seen in the city since the first lock was built at Naburn in 1757. (*Barrie Laws Collection*)

A 1952 picture of the steam towing barge *Ouse* moored at Woods' Albion Wharf. It spent most weekends tied up at this part of Queen's Staithe on the west bank of the Ouse below Ouse Bridge. The late Dick Cressey captained the vessel, bringing barges to York at least twice each week between 1946 and its departure from the river in 1957. Dick lived aboard throughout the week, often leaving York in the early hours to catch the tide below Naburn, picking up on the way the lighters that had discharged on the Foss which had been brought down that river to Blue Bridge. *Ouse* itself loaded 25 tons of coal at York as bunkers and occasionally carried about 60 tons of cargo. (*R.W. Cowl*)

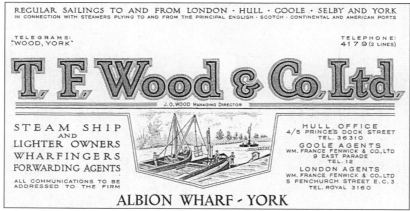

A letterhead used in the 1930s by T.F. Wood & Co., owners of several inland waterway craft, including *Ouse*, that traded to York. In the first half of the twentieth century, the company brought general cargo such as strawboard, timber, cattlefood and flour up to the city. They also brought raw sugar for the sugar factories established in the 1920s at Selby and Poppleton, above York, as well as tobacco to Leeds and woodpulp to Barnsley. Additionally, Woods carried a large variety of products for Rowntrees, the chocolate manufacturers, comprising cocoa beans, sultanas, sugar, gum arabic, nuts, milk powder, pineapples, cherries and fruit essences. Terrys, York's other chocolate manufacturers, similarly received these cargoes from Woods' craft until 1925 in the days when they had a wharf near Skeldergate Bridge.

Activity at Queen's Staithe in June 1971 as sacks of cocoa beans are transferred from barge to dray. (*Sheila Nix Collection*)

19 October 1982 saw the final flurry of barge activity in York as fifteen vessels arrived. Twelve were loaded with cocoa beans, two with paper and one with fuel oil. This photograph of craft at Queen's Staithe was taken in the late 1970s at an earlier occurrence of this type of spasmodic traffic to the city which usually followed the arrival in Hull of a shipment of cocoa beans for Rowntrees. (*Waterways Museum, Goole*)

King's Staithe on the east bank of the river below Ouse Bridge was once also busy with barge traffic and here, the sloop *Ousefleet*, owned by Williamsons the brickmakers, of Market Weighton, is transferring a cargo of bricks to lorry in the 1930s. Such craft loaded above Bawtry Road Bridge on the Selby Canal or at Broomfleet on the Market Weighton Canal and sailed on the Ouse except for the Selby to York stretch where, like *Prato*, they used the towing service to come upriver; the tides and twisting course of the river making sailing difficult. Two loads per week were usually managed when loading at Selby.

A 1950s view of craft, including Barracloughs' *John William* and *Phyllis*, moored at King's Staithe taken from Ouse Bridge. Woods' premises, which bore the exhortation 'Use the Ouse' for several decades, may be seen across river on Queen's Staithe. *(Vic Dickenson Collection)*

Also taken from Ouse Bridge is this June 1976 view of Whitakers' dry cargo barge *Selebian* which was built as a dumb barge by Connells and spent the depression years of the 1930s lying unfinished on their slip at Selby. Eventually it was completed and bought. An engine was fitted after the vessel had subsequently been purchased by Whitakers. Thousands of tons of demerera sugar were discharged annually about this time at both King's and Queen's Staithes for delivery by lorry to the 1926-built sugar factory above the city. The King's Arms pub, visible in the centre of the picture, is regularly flooded by the Ouse and water completely covered the ground floor windows in October 2000. *(R.W. Cowl)*

Transport by inland waterway has considerable advantages and here, Alan Oliver's workboats are taking rubble away from the site and delivering new construction materials for a riverside redevelopment of the former *Yorkshire Evening Press* premises above Ouse Bridge where access by other means was not practicable.

One of Blundy, Clark & Co.'s vessels at their North Street wharf in 1933. The company used their craft to carry West Riding coal, cement from Hull, and river-dredged aggregate to York, until they moved away from the river in 1962. Premises along this stretch of the river were badly damaged in the Baedeker bombing raids of April 1942; so-called because Hitler was supposed to have retaliated after the Allied bombing of the scenic German city of Lubeck by consulting that company's travel guide to select British targets which included York, Bath, Exeter and Norwich. (*Hugh Murray Collection*)

Also damaged in these air raids of 1942 was Rowntrees' Factory above Blundy, Clarks' Wharf, shown in this 1947 downstream view taken from York's Guildhall, itself hit at the same time. The company, founded here in 1861, repaired the damage and continued to use the premises, though barge-discharging facilities had been transferred to their Navigation Warehouse on the Foss by this time. The remains of a riverside hoist assembly are visible.

A postcard view of York's Guildhall taken from Lendal Bridge in the 1930s as *Reklaw* heads downriver with another load of river-dredged sand for its owners' wharf on the Foss. The Guildhall was built in 1446. Stone from Tadcaster used in the construction of York Minster was landed here and taken through the arch on the riverside. Lendal Bridge was opened in 1863 to replace a ferry crossing. (*Hugh Murray Collection*)

A clinker-built keel is shown on this postcard view moored at Marygate Landing on the Ouse's east bank with a horse and dray probably having collected part of its cargo. In the 1920s, many cargoes of bricks were unloaded from sloops by hand here or at King's Staithe. The bricks were lifted off three at a time, with the cargo of 30,000 plus discharged in a day.

Eight

Above York

An upriver view of a laden keel on the Ouse at York above Scarborough Bridge. Railway signals and a signal box indicate the position of the East Coast main line. *(Hugh Murray Collection)*

This downriver view of the Ouse at Clifton Scalp featured on a postcard used in the 1900s, shows York Corporation's dredging plant at work with one of their steam tugs in attendance. Commercial traffic here was rather sparse even at this time, though a sand barge and a vessel loaded with timber are visible. A ferry crossed the river at this point, overlooked by Government House on the left bank, and there were rowing boats for hire on the right bank; a popular picnic spot. All these are long gone and a 1963-built road crossing now dominates the site.

A bridge to carry York's Northern by-pass road was built in 1986 at Clifton and huge quantities of Trent aggregate were brought over eighty miles by water to the site. Here, *Risby* waits to discharge its cargo whilst the grab on the west bank has begun to off-load *Bonby*. Both craft were owned by John Dean at this time.

Walkers' *Reklaw* was sold in 1981 but continued to win sand from the river bed. The vessel is shown in 1987 doing just that near Nunmonkton at the mouth of the River Nidd. The vessel was sold in 1992 for conversion into a holiday boat for the disabled.

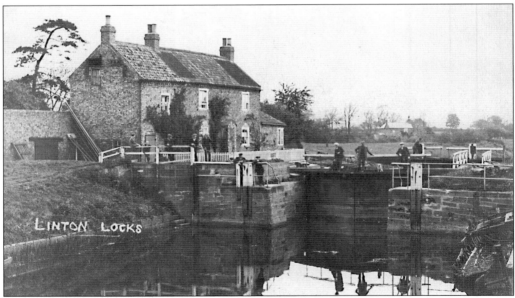

The highest lock and weir on the Ouse are situated at Linton. They were built in the late eighteenth century to improve access to Boroughbridge and Ripon, though commercial traffic above York has never been heavy. The 59ft x 15½ft lock and lockkeeper's house are shown on this 1920s postcard view. Declared unsafe, the lock was closed in 1960 and only reopened after the financial intervention of local pleasure boating enthusiasts.

Blundy, Clark & Co. used to have an extensive sand-winning operation near Boroughbridge. Potters took over the business in 1964 and their *Catherine Clark* is shown approaching Milby Lock in September 1983 loaded with a cargo won from the mouth of the River Swale. The lower River Ure/Milby Cut junction is visible beyond the barge. This traffic finished about 1990. On one occasion in the 1930s, when working above Clifton, one of Blundy Clarks' vessels broke free from its overnight moorings to make an unmanned voyage downriver beneath York's bridges, over Naburn Weir and on to Selby where it sank against the Toll Bridge.

Milby Lock and canal cut at Boroughbridge were built at the same time and for the same reason as Linton Lock and by-passed a stretch of the River Ure. Blundy Clarks were the main users during the twentieth century and one of their vessels is shown being poled and hand-hauled out of the lock after penning up from the river.

127

It would be fitting to end this book with a scene of commercial craft at Ripon, the furthest point north on the Ouse navigation system, However only derelict wharves seem to have featured on photographs, as no cargoes came here in the twentieth century, though sand was delivered to a wharf near Ripon Racecourse, below the town, in the 1920s. This northernmost scene of commercial activity dates from September 1938 and shows Blundy, Clarks' *Catherine Clark* towing their dumb barge *Enid Clark* downriver past pleasure craft moored on the River Ure and into Milby Cut where their owners' wharf is situated. Both craft will probably have loaded sand dredged from the unnavigable Ure near Ripon and come to Boroughbridge via Westwick Lock. (*Pat Jones Collection*)

Acknowledgements

I have used Baron F. Duckham's exemplary book *The Yorkshire Ouse*, published in 1967, for historical detail but the text owes much to Brian Masterman, a mine of information on Goole's docks and shipping; Lawrie Dews, a boatman who spent nearly fifty years with the Selby oil mills' fleets; and the late Dick Cressey, a longtime employee of T.F. Wood & Co. who captained several of their York-based craft.

Brian Masterman has also been most helpful in providing illustrations and I have been allowed to select prints from the collections of Hugh Murray, Sheila Nix and Richard Moody. Eileen Fenteman has kindly allowed me to have access to photographs taken by her late father, Fred Harland; Mrs M. Lobley gave me some of her late husband's slides; and Philip Burnitt, son of the Goole photographer Norman Burnitt, has provided prints from some of his father's negatives.

I am grateful to all the above and to others who have either contributed or helped me track down the illustrations used.